The AntiChrist

Larry D. Harper

The
Elijah
Project

Mesquite, Texas

The AntiChrist
2nd Edition
New Matter Copyright © 1992, 2003 by The Elijah Project
Mesquite, Texas

ISBN 1-880761-06-8

Address all correspondence to:
The Elijah Project
P.O. Box 870153
Mesquite, Texas 75150

Printed in the United States of America

Preface to *The AntiChrist*

The information in this book has been condensed from *The Advent of Christ and AntiChrist* in order to make some of the information in that book available to a wider audience. I thought that only right, since I have chosen to make *The Advent of Christ and AntiChrist* available only to the monthly contributors of *The Voice of Elijah*. The two months that went into the publication of *The Advent of Christ and AntiChrist* gave my life new direction. I pray the time spent reading this condensed version will do the same for you.

I have followed the calling of God I received on the afternoon of August 17, 1966, for over a quarter of a century now, and I thought I was prepared for whatever He would have me do. I was wrong. The understanding of my ministry that I gained while researching and writing *The Advent of Christ and AntiChrist* has totally astounded me. I had no idea such information was ever known to Christian Believers.

Over the past eighteen years (since late April 1974), I have *gradually* understood *what* I was supposed to do to fulfill my calling. But I have never had even so much as a vague inkling as to *why*. Now I know *why* God would have me *restore The Apostolic Teaching* the Church lost so long ago. It is for the benefit of True Believers who must face down Satan as he seeks to stamp out the last bit of God's truth that remains in this realm. That knowledge has given me a renewed diligence, a new desire to do all I possibly can to explain for you what God has done in hiding the Gospel message of Jesus Christ in His Word.

These are not normal times. These are the End Times. Our generation has been selected to witness the final awesome battle between the forces of *Light* and the forces of *Darkness*. We have been chosen to witness the ultimate triumph of good over evil. "Those who have insight" will understand and appreciate the significance of the events that lead up to that great *Day of the Lord*. They will know, almost to the exact day, when the Prince of Darkness enters this realm to make his final stand against the Almighty God. They will also be waiting a few short years later when the Lord of Glory returns for His own.

After you have finished reading what you find written here, I ask that you do but one thing. Just ask yourself, "Do I believe this?" If you do believe, there is much more information to be found in *The Advent of Christ and AntiChrist*. That book is not available for purchase, but if you will become a monthly contributor to *The Voice of Elijah*, I'll send you a copy as my gift to you. Please join with those of us who are already contributing our time and money to reach those who need to know and understand what you already know. Time is running out. Tomorrow may be too late.

August 29, 1992

Preface to the Second Edition

A lot of water has flowed under the proverbial bridge since this booklet came off the press nearly eleven years ago, but nothing much has changed in regard to my understanding of the things the Early Church Fathers Irenæus and Hippolytus recorded more than 1,800 years ago. If anything, since the events of 9/11/01, their statements concerning the Antichrist have come into even clearer focus.

May 19, 2003

CONTENTS

INTRODUCTION

The following pages contain two separate works on the subject of the AntiChrist and the Second Coming of Jesus Christ. The first is that of the Church Father Irenæus (A.D. 120–202). The second is the work of his disciple Hippolytus (A.D. 170–236). For both of these works I have used the century-old English translation one can find in *The Ante–Nicene Fathers* edited by Alexander Roberts and James Donaldson.

The works of these two men should not be, as they have been, casually dismissed as the irrelevant rambling of the primitive mind. It is true they contain statements that seem "unsophisticated" to our way of thinking. Yet many of these apparently unsophisticated statements are extremely precise and to the point. They were made by men who had a fairly accurate understanding of the prophetic message of the Old Testament. We do not understand what they wrote today simply because we are victims of the working of Satan, whereby he successfully led the Church astray from the apostolic tradition—what I call *The Teaching*—and into a theology based on Greek philosophical concepts. While that philosophically based theology was able to preserve the basic doctrines of Christianity, *The Apostolic Teaching* can be fully understood and communicated accurately only by thinking and speaking in terms of the *parabolic imagery* in which it was originally given by the Old Testament Prophets. I have already begun to *restore* the *parabolic* basis for *The Teaching* in the volumes of the Resurrection Theology Series. Those of you who are familiar with what I have presented there can better appreciate what these men have written.

The absolute agreement between Irenæus and Hippolytus that there is but one accurate understanding of the Scriptures provides an automatic indictment of anyone who challenges what they have written. Moreover, anyone who rejects their understanding has also done little more than confess an obvious ignorance of second-century Christianity in general and the work of Irenæus in particular. Such a person must carry the label "heretic" simply because the Early Church Father Irenæus defined that term in his monumental second-century work, *Against Heresies*.[1]

The very basis of Irenæus' five volume *Against Heresies* is that the leaders of the Church knew but one *oral tradition*, and that *oral tradition* had been *delivered* to them by the Apostles. He vehemently argued that anyone who disagreed with the *oral tradition* of the Church was, by definition, a heretic. So anyone today who contends he was wrong in what he has written has thereby sided with the Gnostics and other second-century heretical sects in denying that Christian theology had any essential content to begin with. What does that make those who disagree with Irenæus? Heretics all.

Irenæus was a disciple of Polycarp, who had been a disciple of the Apostle John. Both he and Polycarp believed they had been

---

[1]The Greek term *hæresis* literally *means* "school of thought." At the time Irenæus appropriated the term, it was commonly used to refer to any of the Greek philosophical schools of thought, without any negative connotation. The Jewish historian Josephus, writing sometime in the late first century, applied the term to the Pharisees, Saduccees, and Essenes, endeavoring to elevate these three sects of Judaism to the same intellectual position as the Greek Stoics. He did so hoping to gain for the Jews a more favorable view in the eyes of educated people. (See E. Rivkin, *A Hidden Revolution*, Abingdon: Nashville, 1978, pp. 31 ff.) This illustrates how before Irenæus' use of the term, it had no perjorative sense. Irenæus intentionally gave it one in the Christian vocabulary. In fact, his view of Christianity is aptly demonstrated by his appropriation of this one term: "Unbelievers have their schools of thought (*hæreseis*), each with its own disciples (*mathetes*) and its own tradition (*paradosis*). Christianity also has disciples (*mathetes*) and a tradition (*paradosis*). However, Christianity is not a school of thought (*hæresis*) because the apostolic tradition was divinely revealed to the Apostles. So it is not the product of human thought processes. The heretics have made the apostolic tradition a school of thought (*hæresis*) by changing it to suit themselves. Therefore, the difference between the Church and Christian heresies (*hæreseis*) is obvious. The Church does not change the apostolic tradition. The heretics do." His argument discloses how much the Church has lost.

accurately taught the *apostolic tradition*. Irenæus wrote this of his Teacher Polycarp:[2]

> But **Polycarp also was not only instructed by apostles**, and conversed with many who had seen Christ, but was also, by apostles in Asia, appointed bishop of the Church in Smyrna, whom I also saw in my early youth, for he tarried [on earth] a very long time, and, when a very old man, gloriously and most nobly suffering martyrdom, departed this life, *always taught the things which he had learned from the apostles, and which the Church has handed down, and which alone are true.*
> (*Against Heresies*, III, 4)

Finally, Hippolytus, the author of the other work I have included, was a disciple of Irenæus. You will find in his works that he too believed he had been accurately taught those things the Apostles *received* from Jesus Christ by revelation.

The writings of Irenæus and Hippolytus disclose they clearly believed their obligation as disciples and Teachers in the Church was first to master *The Apostolic Teaching* and then to transmit it unchanged to a subsequent generation. They appear to have succeeded quite well in that endeavor. How then did the Church lose *The Teaching*?[3] I have explained generally how that happened in *The Way, The Truth, The Life*.[4] And for several years now, I have been explaining specifics in the pages of *The Voice of Elijah Update*. I plan to explain even more in future volumes of *The Mystery of Scripture*.

Irenæus and Hippolytus agree on all the basic points regarding the advent of Christ and the AntiChrist, although Hippolytus provides somewhat more detail. The beliefs these two held in common can be briefly summarized as follows:

1. Satan will appear as a man in the person of the AntiChrist because he seeks to reign as king over mankind and desires to focus the worship of God on himself.

---

[2]The translation provided is that found in *The Ante-Nicene Fathers*, Editors A. Roberts & J. Donaldson as reprinted by Wm. B. Eerdmans (Grand Rapids: 1973).

[3]See "The Protestant Confession: The Church Lost *The Teaching*" in *The Voice of Elijah*, January 1992.

[4]Larry D. Harper, *The Way, The Truth, The Life*, Second edition, The Elijah Project (Mesquite, TX: 1999)

2. The AntiChrist will be a Jew, and will achieve his stated objectives by being accepted as the Christ, the messianic king of the Jews, taking his seat in the rebuilt temple in Jerusalem, pretending to be God Himself, and thereby becoming the "abomination of desolation" spoken of by the prophet Daniel and mentioned also by Jesus.[5]

3. The AntiChrist is the "little horn" of the fourth beast mentioned in Daniel 7. He will slay three of the other horns[6] and reign as an eighth with the remaining seven.

4. The AntiChrist will achieve his objectives in the middle of the final seven-year period of this age. At that time he will be proclaimed the messianic king of the Jews and will take his seat as God in the rebuilt temple in Jerusalem. He will reign for three and one-half years.

5. The AntiChrist, during his reign, will deceive the majority of people living on the Earth at the time into believing he is God. However, he will persecute those who refuse to worship him because they are able to see through his delusion.

6. Jesus Christ will return to Earth at the end of the three and one-half year reign of the AntiChrist, destroying Satan's kingdom. The resurrection of the just will occur at that time.

Perhaps the most significant thing about the understanding that Irenæus and Hippolytus had concerning the advent of Jesus Christ and that of the AntiChrist is the absolute conviction that what they believed was true. Their conviction came from the knowledge that they had *received* an accurate explanation of the Apostles' understanding of the message of Scripture which had been *handed down* by the Apostle John to Polycarp. That provided them a much more solid basis for their beliefs than the rambling speculation one finds in current books on biblical prophecy. Therefore, perhaps you should seriously consider the basis for your own beliefs rather than hastily discarding the sources you find assembled here. If you do otherwise, you may well find yourself lacking crucial information at that most important time. But, no matter what you do as an individual, the righteous will be ready when Jesus Christ returns. As Jesus said, "Wisdom is vindicated by her deeds."[7]

---

[5]Daniel 12:11; Matthew 24:15.
[6]Hippolytus explains that those three are the rulers of Egypt, Libya, and Ethiopia.
[7]Matthew 11:19.

IRENÆUS:
Against Heresies (V, 19–30)

CHAPTER XIX

2. The heretics,[8] being all unlearned and ignorant of God's arrangements, and not acquainted with that dispensation by which He took upon Him human nature, inasmuch as they blind themselves with regard to the truth, do in fact speak against their own salvation. Some of them introduce another Father besides the Creator. Some, again, say that the world and its substance was made by certain angels.

Certain others [maintain] that it was widely separated by Horos from him whom they represent as being the Father—that it sprang forth of itself, and from itself was born. Then, again, others [of them assert] that it obtained substance in those things which are contained by the Father, from defect and ignorance. Others still, despise the advent of the Lord manifest [to the senses], for they do not admit His incarnation; while others, ignoring the arrangement [that He should be born] of a virgin, maintain that He was begotten by Joseph.

And still further, some affirm that neither their soul nor their body can receive eternal life, but merely the inner man. Moreover, they will have it that this [inner man] is that which is the understanding in them, and which they decree as being the only thing to

---

[8]By "heretics" Irenæus *means* those who claim to be Christian but aren't simply because they do not adhere to the apostolic tradition. Early on, many of those who made counterfeit claims of legitimacy challenged *The Teaching* of the Church, claiming to have a more complete understanding of the message of the Scriptures, or claiming that only one of the Apostles accurately understood the Old Testament message (cf. 1 Cor. 1:10–17).

ascend to "the perfect." Others [maintain], as I have said in the first book, that while the soul is saved, their body does not participate in the salvation which comes from God; in which [book] I have also set forward the hypotheses of all these men, and in the second have pointed out their weakness and inconsistency.

CHAPTER XX

1. Now *all these [heretics] are of much later date than the bishops to whom the apostles committed the Churches;*[9] which fact I have in the third book taken all pains to demonstrate. It follows, then, as a matter of course, that these heretics aforementioned, since they are blind to the truth, and deviate from *the [right] way,* will walk in various roads; and therefore the footsteps of their doctrine are scattered here and there *without agreement or connection.*[10]

But *the path* of those belonging to the Church circumscribes the whole world, as *possessing the sure tradition from the apostles*, and gives unto us to see that *the faith of all is one and the same,*[11] since all receive one and the same God the Father, and believe in the same dispensation regarding the incarnation of the Son of God, and are cognizant of the same gift of the Spirit, and are conversant with the same commandments, and present the same form of ecclesiastical constitution, and expect the same advent of the Lord, and await the

---

[9]Irenæus always puts forward the same argument to refute the heretics' claim to the title "Christian." It can be summarized succinctly: "The Church *received The Teaching* as an *oral tradition handed down* from the Apostles. That *oral tradition—The Teaching*—existed in the Churches long before the heretics' distortions of it arose. Therefore, *The Teaching* holds the primacy of position among Church leaders. While the Apostles and the Church leaders they appointed have always agreed there is but one truth, the heretics fail to agree on much at all. Consequently, the *oral tradition* of the Apostles distinguishes itself through the agreement of Church leaders." Irenæus' argument in refutation of heretics is, because of its adamant appeal to the Church's one common teaching, an eye-opening disclosure of just how far down the Church has come to its present state.

[10]Irenæus is now going to contrast the teaching of the heretics with *The Teaching* of the Church. His point is, the Church's *Teaching* does have "agreement and connection."

[11]This summarizes his argument against heretics. By "faith" he *means* "belief."

same salvation of the complete man, that is, of the soul and body.

And undoubtedly *the preaching of the Church is true and stead-fast, in which one and the same way of salvation is shown throughout the whole world*. For to her is entrusted *the light of God*; and therefore the "wisdom" of God, by means of which she saves all men,

> "is declared in [its] going forth; it uttereth [its voice] faithfully in the streets, is preached on the tops of the walls, and speaks continually in the gates of the city."
> (Proverbs 1:20–21)

For the Church preaches *the truth*[12] everywhere, and she is the seven-branched candlestick which bears *the light of Christ*.

2. *Those, therefore, who desert the preaching of the Church, call in question the knowledge of the holy presbyters*, not taking into consideration of how much greater consequence is a religious man, even in a private station, than a blasphemous and impudent sophist. Now, such are all the heretics, and those who imagine that they have hit upon something more beyond *the truth*,[13] so that by following those

---

[12]Irenæus has no doubt the Church of his day understood the truth concerning the message of the Old Testament Gospel of Jesus Christ. He is equally as confident the heretics have no such understanding.

[13]This statement discloses why the Church lost *The Apostolic Teaching*. Individuals who did not truly believe *The Teaching* were not content with *handing down* what they had been taught. They discovered their position of leadership in the Church became much more gratifying if they could from time to time share some of their own personal insight into the Scriptures. Before long others followed their example and all too soon the fires of Gnosticism (which is just another way of saying "speculation") raged through the Church. Irenæus and others, like Hippolytus and another Church leader named Tertullian, sought to refute the heretics by appealing to the apostolic tradition. Together these three—some of the most prominent leaders in the Early Church—sought to "build a fence around *The Teaching*" as it were. They were somewhat successful. But eventually, as those Church leaders who knew *The Teaching* died, untrained leaders replaced them, and the Church lost more and more specific understanding of *The Teaching*. Finally, Greek philosophy supplanted the *parabolic imagery* and Hebrew idioms in which the apostolic tradition was grounded. The death-knell for *The Teaching* as an apostolic tradition was sounded when a Church leader named Origen (ca. A.D. 200) began teaching allegorical interpretation as a way for individuals to interpret the Scriptures for themselves. (See *The Mystery of Scripture*.)

things already mentioned, *proceeding on their way variously, inharmoniously, and foolishly, not keeping always to the same opinions with regard to the same things, as blind men are led by the blind, they shall deservedly fall into the ditch of ignorance lying in their path,*[14] *ever seeking and never finding out the truth.*[15]

It behoves us, therefore, to avoid their doctrines, and to take careful heed lest we suffer any injury from them; but to flee to the Church, and be brought up in her bosom, and be nourished with the Lord's Scriptures. For the Church has been planted as a garden in this world; therefore says the Spirit of God, "Thou mayest freely eat from every tree of the garden,"[16] that is, Eat ye from every Scripture of the Lord; but ye shall not eat with an uplifted mind, nor touch any heretical discord.

For these men do profess that they have themselves the knowledge of good and evil; and they set their own impious minds above the God who made them. *They therefore form opinions on what is*

---

[14]Notice his allusion to Jesus' ridicule of the Scribes and Pharisees for their ignorance of the true *meaning* of the Scriptures (Matthew 23:16 ff.).

[15]He is alluding to 2 Timothy 3:7. Irenæus has aptly described the Church of today. No one Church leader completely agrees with another because everyone bases his knowledge of the Scriptural message on his own inherent capabilities as an intellectual being. Each one reserves the right to construct his own version of the "truth." By contrast, God revealed *The Teaching* to the Apostles, who passed it along unchanged to the next generation of Church leaders, who passed it on (changed somewhat, unfortunately) to the next, etc. Consider the evidence: Irenæus understood much of *The Teaching*. Therefore, he based his refutation of heretics on the fact that the apostolic tradition begun by the revelation Jesus Christ had given to His disciples (Luke 24:45) was still alive and functioning in the Church in his own day. Hence, he could argue that all the Church leaders who understood *The Teaching* agreed as to its content. Those who disagreed did so because they were unwilling to submit to a divinely appointed Teacher and be taught. They were too busy playing the proverbial fool, wanting only to reveal the idiocy of their own thinking. The majority in the Church today fall into that same category. They fail to understand the true "disciple" in God's view is a *learner*. What did God intend the disciples of Jesus Christ to *learn* if He did not provide it in *The Teaching* of Jesus Christ? (See "Where Are Jesus' Disciples?" in *The Voice of Elijah*, April 1991.)

[16]Genesis 2:16.

beyond the limits of the understanding. For this cause also the apostle says, "Be not wise beyond what it is fitting to be wise, but be wise prudently,"[17] that we be not cast forth by eating of the "knowledge" of these men (that knowledge which knows more than it should do) from the paradise of life.

Into this paradise the Lord has introduced those who obey His call, "summing up in Himself all things which are in heaven, and which are on earth;"[18] but the things in heaven are spiritual, while those on earth constitute the dispensation in human nature. These things, therefore, He recapitulated in Himself: by uniting man to the Spirit, and causing the Spirit to dwell in man. He is Himself made the head of the Spirit, and gives the Spirit to be the head of man: for through Him (the Spirit) we see, and hear, and speak.

CHAPTER XXI

1. He has therefore, in His work of recapitulation, summed up all things, both waging war against our enemy, and crushing him who had at the beginning led us away captives in Adam, and trampled upon his head, as thou canst perceive in Genesis that God said to the serpent,

> "And I will put enmity between thee and the woman, and between thy seed and her seed; He shall be on the watch for[19] thy head, and thou on the watch for His heel."
> (Genesis 3:15)

For from that time, He who should be born of a woman, [namely] from the Virgin, after the likeness of Adam, was preached as keeping watch for the head of the serpent. This is the seed of which the apostle says in the Epistle to the Galatians, "that the law of works was established until the seed should come to whom the promise was made."[20] This fact is exhibited in a still clearer light in

---

[17]Romans 12:3.

[18]Ephesians 1:10.

[19]The misunderstanding here as to the *meaning* of this Scripture was apparently introduced by a translator of the Greek Septuagint who translated the Hebrew verb *shuph* ("to bruise") with the Greek term τηρησει ("to watch").

[20]Galatians 3:19.

the same Epistle, where he thus speaks:

> "But when the fulness of time was come, God sent forth His Son, made of a woman."
> (Galatians 4:4)

For indeed the enemy would not have been fairly vanquished, unless it had been a man [born] of a woman who conquered him. For it was by means of a woman that he got the advantage over man at first, setting himself up as man's opponent. And therefore does the Lord profess Himself to be the Son of man, comprising in Himself that original man out of whom the woman was fashioned, in order that, as our species went down to death through a vanquished man, so we may ascend to life again through a victorious one; and as through a man death received the palm [of victory] against us, so again by a man we may receive the palm against death.

2. Now the Lord would not have recapitulated in Himself that ancient and primary enmity against the serpent, fulfilling the promise of the Creator, and performing His command, if He had come from another Father. But as He is one and the same, who formed us at the beginning, and sent His Son at the end, the Lord did perform His command, being made of a woman, by both destroying our adversary, and perfecting man after the image and likeness of God. And for this reason He did not draw the means of confounding him from any other source than from the words of the law, and made use of the Father's commandment as a help towards the destruction and confusion of the apostate angel.

Fasting forty days, like Moses and Elijah, He afterwards hungered, first, in order that we may perceive that He was a real and substantial man—for it belongs to a man to suffer hunger when fasting; and secondly, that His opponent might have an opportunity of attacking Him. For as at the beginning it was by means of food that [the enemy] persuaded man, although not suffering hunger, to transgress God's commandments, so in the end he did not succeed in persuading Him that was an hungered to take that food which proceeded from God. For, when tempting Him, he said,

> "If thou be the Son of God, command that these stones be made bread."
> (Matthew 4:3)

But the Lord repulsed him by the commandment of the law, saying,

"It is written, Man doth not live by bread alone."
(Deuteronomy 8:3)

As to those words [of His enemy], "If thou be the Son of God," [the Lord] made no remark; but by thus acknowledging His human nature He baffled His adversary, and exhausted the force of his first attack by means of His Father's word. The corruption of man therefore, which occurred in paradise by both [of our first parents] eating, was done away with by [the Lord's] want of food in this world.

But he, being thus vanquished by the law, endeavoured again to make an assault by himself quoting a commandment of the law. For, bringing Him to the highest pinnacle of the temple, he said to Him,

"If thou art the Son of God, cast thyself down. For it is written, That God shall give His angels charge concerning thee, and in their hands they shall bear thee up, lest perchance thou dash thy foot against a stone . . ."
(Psalm 91:11–12)

thus *concealing a falsehood under the guise of Scripture, as is done by all the heretics.*[21] For that was indeed written, [namely], "That He hath given His angels charge concerning Him;" but "cast thyself down from hence" no Scripture said in reference to Him. This kind of persuasion the devil produced from himself. The Lord therefore confuted him out of the law, when He said, "It is written again, Thou shalt not tempt the LORD thy God;"[22] pointing out by the word contained in the law that which is the duty of man, that he should not tempt God; and in regard to Himself, since He appeared in human form, [declaring] that He would not tempt the LORD his God.

The pride of reason, therefore, which was in the serpent, was put to nought by the humility found in the man [Christ], and now twice was the devil conquered from Scripture, when he was detected as advising things contrary to God's commandment, and was shown to be the enemy of God by [the expression of] his

---

[21]Irenæus' purpose in discussing the activity and tactics of Satan will become clearer as he progresses. He intends to show that Satan controls mankind by distorting what God has said in the Hebrew Scriptures. He knows that Satan's ultimate distortion of that truth, however, will be the appearance of the AntiChrist. That is a topic he will introduce shortly.
[22]Deuteronomy 6:16.

thoughts. He then, having been thus signally defeated, and then, as it were, concentrating his forces, drawing up in order all his available power for falsehood in the third place "showed Him all the kingdoms of the world, and the glory of them,"[23] saying, as Luke relates,

> "All these will I give thee,—for they are delivered to me; and to whom I will, I give them,—if thou wilt fall down and worship me."
> (Luke 4:6–7)

The LORD then, exposing him in his true character, says,

> "Depart, Satan; for it is written, Thou shalt worship the Lord thy God, and Him only shalt thou serve."
> (Matthew 4:10)

He both revealed him by this name, and showed [at the same time] who He Himself was.[24] For the Hebrew word "Satan" signifies an apostate. And thus, vanquishing him for the third time, He spurned him from Him finally as being conquered out of the law; and there was done away with that infringement of God's commandment which had occurred in Adam, by means of the precept of the law, which the Son of man observed, who did not transgress the commandment of God.

3. Who, then, is this Lord God to whom Christ bears witness, whom no man shall tempt, whom all should worship, and serve Him alone? It is, beyond all manner of doubt, that God who also gave the law. For these things had been predicted in the law, and by the words of the law the Lord showed that the law does indeed declare the Word of God from the Father; and the apostate angel of God is destroyed by its voice, being exposed in his true colours, and vanquished by the Son of man keeping the commandment of God.

For as in the beginning he enticed man to transgress his Maker's law, and thereby got him into his power; yet his power con-

---

[23]Luke 4:5.

[24]This is a reference to Satan's ignorance concerning God's plan. Satan does not always understand what God intends to do, as is presently his primary consternation. He recognized Jesus as the Messiah only when he saw Him baptized by John the Baptist—when the Spirit descended on Him accompanied by God's declaration that He was His Son (Matt. 3:13–17). Even then Satan was not absolutely certain who Jesus was until Jesus revealed His Own knowledge of Satan's identity, thus confirming for him that God had taken up residence in human flesh.

sists in transgression and apostasy, and with these he bound man [to himself]; so again, on the other hand, it was necessary that through man himself he should, when conquered, be bound with the same chains with which he had bound man, in order that man, being set free, might return to his Lord, leaving to him (Satan) those bonds by which he himself had been fettered, that is, sin. For *when Satan is bound, man is set free*; since

> "none can enter a strong man's house and spoil his goods, unless he first bind the strong man himself."
> (Matthew 12:29; Mark 3:27)

The Lord therefore exposes him as speaking contrary to the word of that God who made all things, and subdues him by means of the commandment. Now the law is the commandment of God. *The Man*[25] proves him to be a fugitive from and a transgressor of the law, an apostate also from God. After [*the Man* had done this], the Word bound him securely as a fugitive from Himself, and made spoil of his goods,—namely, those men whom he held in bondage, and whom he unjustly used for his own purposes. And justly indeed is he led captive, who had led men unjustly into bondage; while man, who had been led captive in times past, was rescued from the grasp of his possessor, according to the tender mercy of God the Father, who had compassion on His own handiwork, and gave to it salvation, restoring it by means of the Word—that is, by Christ—in order that men might learn by actual proof that he receives incorruptibility not of himself, but by the free gift of God.

CHAPTER XXII

1. Thus then does the Lord plainly show that it was the true Lord and the one God who had been set forth by the law; for Him whom the law proclaimed as God, the same did Christ point out as the Father, whom also it behoves the disciples of Christ alone to

---

[25]When I wrote the comments for the first edition, I did not yet understand the *significance* of Irenæus' reference to Jesus Christ as "*The Man*." Since that time, I have come to understand how Moses concealed the Truth of what he wrote about Jesus Christ by that subterfuge. (See "He's Coming in Clouds of Glory (Whatever That Means)" *The Voice of Elijah*, January 2001 and "Questions & Answers," *The Voice of Elijah*, July 2001, for an explanation of those things.) That is what Irenæus is referring to here.

serve. By means of the statements of the law, He put our adversary to utter confusion;[26] and the law directs us to praise God the Creator, and to serve Him alone. Since this is the case, we must not seek for another Father besides Him, or above Him, since there is one God who justifies the circumcision by faith, and the uncircumcision through faith.[27]

For if there were any other perfect Father above Him, He (Christ) would by no means have overthrown Satan by means of His words and commandments. For one ignorance cannot be done away with by means of another ignorance, any more than one defect by another defect.[28] If, therefore, the law is due to ignorance and defect, how could the statements contained therein bring to nought the ignorance of the devil, and conquer the strong man? For a strong man can be conquered neither by an inferior nor by an equal, but by one possessed of greater power.

But the Word of God is the superior above all, He who is loudly proclaimed in the law: "Hear, O Israel, the LORD thy God is one God;" and,

> "Thou shalt love the LORD thy God with all thy heart;" and, "Him shalt thou adore, and Him alone shalt thou serve."
> (Deuteronomy 6:4–5, 13)

Then in the Gospel, casting down the apostasy by means of these expressions, He did both overcome the strong man by His Father's voice, and He acknowledges the commandment of the law to express His own sentiments, when He says, "Thou shalt not tempt the LORD thy God." For He did not confound the adversary by the saying of any other, but by that belonging to His own Father, and thus overcame the strong man.

* * * * * * *[29]

---

[26]Satan would rather we not understand this about him. He has power, but his greatest power is his ability to persuade fools to believe something other than the Truth.

[27]Romans 3:30.

[28]Irenæus is still refuting the Gnostics. They claimed sin came into the world through a mistake of its creator, who was a lesser god.

[29]In the two chapters omitted here, Irenæus explains that Satan is a liar, constantly striving to deceive us. In support of his explanation, he quotes John 8:44, where Jesus says Satan "is a liar, and the father of lies."

CHAPTER XXV

1. And not only by the particulars already mentioned, but also *by means of the events which shall occur in the time of Antichrist is it shown that he, being an apostate and a robber, is anxious to be adored as God*; and that, although a mere slave, *he wishes himself to be proclaimed as a king.*[30] For he (Antichrist) being endued with all the power of the devil, shall come, not as a righteous king, nor as a legitimate king, [i.e., one] in subjection to God, but an impious, unjust, and lawless one; as an apostate, iniquitous and murderous; as a robber, concentrating, in himself [all] satanic apostasy, and *setting aside idols to persuade [men] that he himself is God*, raising up himself as the only idol, having in himself the multifarious errors of the other idols. This he does, in order that they who do [now] worship the devil by means of many abominations, may serve himself by this one idol, of whom the apostle thus speaks in the second Epistle to the Thessalonians:

> "Unless there shall come a falling away first, and the man of sin shall be revealed, the son of perdition, who opposeth and exalteth himself above all that is called God, or that is worshipped; so that he sitteth in the temple of God, showing himself as if he were God." (2 Thessalonians 2:3–4)

The apostle therefore clearly points out his apostasy, and that he is lifted up above all that is called God, or that is worshipped— that is, above every idol—for these are indeed so called by men, but are not [really] gods; and that *he will endeavour in a tyrannical manner to set himself forth as God.*[31]

2. Moreover, he (the apostle) has also pointed out this which I have shown in many ways, that the temple in Jerusalem[32] was

---

[30]Here Irenæus is specific. The AntiChrist will be Satan in human form. And his purpose in becoming the AntiChrist is to fulfill his longing to reign as king over men and be worshipped as God.

[31]Notice that Satan sets himself forth as not just any god, but as the God of Abraham, Isaac, and Jacob. He will accomplish that by sitting in the temple of God in Jerusalem.

[32]Note what Irenæus is saying. He says the Apostle Paul was speaking concerning the temple in Jerusalem when he says the AntiChrist would take his seat "in the temple." Yet when Irenæus wrote this, the temple in Jerusalem had been destroyed for over a century. Therefore, he knew the temple had to be rebuilt. The same circumstance remains true today. But not for long.

made by the direction of the true God. For the apostle himself, speaking in his own person, distinctly called it the temple of God.

Now I have shown in the third book, that no one is termed God by the apostles when speaking for themselves, except Him who truly is God, the Father of our Lord, by whose directions the temple which is at Jerusalem was constructed for those purposes which I have already mentioned; *in which [temple] the enemy shall sit, endeavouring to show himself as Christ,*[33] as the Lord also declares:

> "But when ye shall see *the abomination of desolation*, which has been spoken of by Daniel the prophet, standing in the holy place (let him that readeth understand), then let those who are in Judea flee into the mountains; and he who is upon the house-top, let him not come down to take anything out of his house: for there shall then be great hardship, such as has not been from the beginning of the world until now, nor ever shall be."[34]
> (Matthew 24:15–21)

3. Daniel too, looking forward to the end of the last kingdom, i.e., the ten last kings, amongst whom the kingdom of those men shall be partitioned, and upon whom the son of perdition shall come, declares that ten horns shall spring from the beast, and that another little horn shall arise in the midst of them, and that three of the former shall be rooted up before his face. He says:

> "And, behold, eyes were in this horn as the eyes of a man, and a mouth speaking great things, and his look was more stout than his fellows. I was looking, and this horn made war against the saints, and prevailed against them until the Ancient of days came and gave judgment to the saints of the most high God, and the time came, and the saints obtained the kingdom."
> (Daniel 7:8, 21–22)

Then, further on, in the interpretation of the vision, there was said to him:

> "The fourth beast shall be the fourth kingdom upon earth, which shall excel all other kingdoms, and devour the whole earth, and tread it down, and cut it in pieces. And its ten horns are ten kings

---

[33]He quickly passes over what is most significant for our own time: Satan will come pretending to be Jesus Christ, the Messiah of the Jews.
[34]Take heed. The "abomination of desolation" Jesus mentions in Matthew 24:15 is Satan sitting on the throne of God in the Holy of Holies in the rebuilt temple in Jerusalem, being hailed as the Messiah of the Jews.

which shall arise; and after them shall arise another, who shall sur-
pass in evil deeds all that were before him, and shall overthrow
three kings; and he shall speak words against the most high God,
and wear out the saints of the most high God, and shall purpose to
change times and laws; and [everything] shall be given into his
hand until a time of times and a half time."
(Daniel 7:23–25)

that is, *for three years and six months, during which time, when he
comes, he shall reign over the earth.* Of whom also the Apostle Paul
again, speaking in the second [Epistle] to the Thessalonians, and at
the same time proclaiming *the cause of his advent*,[35] thus says:

"And then shall the wicked one be revealed, whom the Lord Jesus
shall slay with the spirit of His mouth, and destroy by the presence
of His coming; whose coming [i.e., the wicked one's] is after the
working of Satan, in all power, and signs, and portents of lies, and
with all deceivableness of wickedness for those who perish; *because
they did not receive the love of the truth, that they might be saved.
And therefore God will send them the working of error, that they may
believe a lie, that they all may be judged who did not believe the truth,*
but gave consent to iniquity."
(2 Thessalonians 2:8–12)

4. The Lord also spoke as follows to those who did not believe
in Him:

"I have come in my Father's name, and ye have not received Me.
When another shall come in his own name, him ye will receive,"[36]
(John 5:43)

---

[35]Understand what Irenæus says. God has a distinct purpose in the
advent of the AntiChrist. Those who have no "love of the truth" will be
taken in by his delusion and will thereby be left without excuse. "The
cause of his advent" is, put simply, God's desire to sift all mankind to
separate the wheat from the chaff, the wheat from the tares. The Apostle
Paul plainly states that the source of the delusion is God Himself.

[36]Jesus spoke these words to the Jews. They will willingly accept "the
other" of whom He spoke. However, the "Christian" Pretenders in the
Church today will also be taken in by the pretense of the AntiChrist and
his awesome demonstration of power because they have been prepared
by those who teach the Dispensational theory of biblical interpretation.
[See "Wanna Hear the Whopper the Liar Came Up With? I Doubt You
Will Believe It!" *The Voice of Elijah*, October 1996.]

calling Antichrist "the other," because he is alienated from the Lord. This is also the unjust judge, whom the Lord mentioned as one "who feared not God, neither regarded man," to whom the widow fled in her forgetfulness of God,—that is, the earthly Jerusalem,—to be avenged of her adversary. Which also he shall do in the time of his kingdom: he shall remove his kingdom into that [city], and shall sit in the temple of God, *leading astray those who worship him, as if he were Christ*. To this purpose Daniel says again:

> "And he shall desolate the holy place; and sin has been given for a sacrifice, and righteousness been cast away in the earth, and he has been active and gone on prosperously."[37]
> (Daniel 8:12)

And the angel Gabriel, when explaining his vision, states with regard to this person:

> "And towards the end of their kingdom a king of a most fierce countenance shall arise, one understanding [dark] questions, and exceedingly powerful, full of wonders; and he shall corrupt, direct, influence, and put strong men down, the holy people likewise; and his yoke shall be directed as a wreath [round their neck]; deceit shall be in his hand, and he shall be lifted up in his heart. He shall also ruin many by deceit, and lead many to perdition, bruising them in his hand like eggs."
> (Daniel 8:23–25)

And then he points out *the time that his tyranny shall last, during which the saints shall be put to flight*, they who offer a pure sacrifice unto God:

> "And in the midst of the week,"

he says,

> "the sacrifice and the libation shall be taken away, and the abomination of desolation [shall be brought] into the temple: even unto the consummation of the time shall the desolation be complete."
> (Daniel 9:27)

---

[37]Here Irenæus uses the words of the Prophet Daniel which predicted the first incarnation of Satan in the person of Antiochus Epiphanes (167 B.C.) to show that they describe the characteristic activity of Satan that we may expect of the AntiChrist in our time also.

Now three years and six months constitute the half-week.

5. From all these passages are revealed to us, not merely the particulars of the apostasy, and [the doings] of him who concentrates in himself every satanic error, but also, that there is one and the same God the Father, who was declared by the prophets, but made manifest by Christ. For if what Daniel prophesied concerning the end has been confirmed by the Lord, when He said,

> "When ye shall see *the abomination of desolation*, which has been spoken of by Daniel the prophet"
> (Matthew 24:15)

(and the angel Gabriel gave the interpretation of the visions to Daniel, and he is the archangel of the Creator, who also proclaimed to Mary the visible coming and the incarnation of Christ), then one and the same God is most manifestly pointed out, who sent the prophets, and made promises of the Son, and called us into His knowledge.

CHAPTER XXVI

1. In a still clearer light has John, in the Apocalypse, indicated to the Lord's disciples what shall happen in the last times, and concerning the ten kings who shall then arise, among whom the empire which now rules [the earth] shall be partitioned.[38] He teaches us what the ten horns shall be which were seen by Daniel,[39] telling us that thus it had been said to him:

> "And the ten horns which thou sawest are ten kings, who have received no kingdom as yet, but shall receive power as if kings one hour with the beast. These have one mind, and give their strength and power to the beast. These shall make war with the Lamb, and the Lamb shall overcome them, because He is the Lord of lords and

---

[38]He understands the Roman Empire of his day issues into the ten horns. He can only be referring to the ten horns of the fourth beast in Daniel 7. He also says those ten horns are ten "kings," not ten "nations."

[39]Irenæus has here identified the ten horns of the scarlet beast described in Revelation 17 with the ten horns on the beast described in Daniel 7. This identification will eventually explain for us how the events described in Revelation 15–18 relate to events described earlier in the Book of Revelation.

the king of kings."
(Revelation 17:12–14)

It is manifest, therefore, that of these [potentates], he who is to come shall slay three, and subject the remainder to his power, and that he shall be himself the eighth among them.[40] And *they shall lay Babylon waste, and burn her with fire, and shall give their kingdom to the beast,*[41] *and put the Church to flight.*[42] After that they shall be destroyed by the coming of our Lord. For that the kingdom must be divided, and thus come to ruin, the Lord [declares when He] says:

> "Every kingdom divided against itself is brought to desolation, and every city or house divided against itself shall not stand."
> (Matthew 12:25)

It must be, therefore, that the kingdom, the city, and the house be divided into ten; and for this reason He has already foreshadowed the partition and division [which shall take place]. Daniel also says particularly, that the end of the fourth kingdom consists in the toes of the image seen by Nebuchadnezzar, upon which came the stone cut out without hands; and as he does himself say:

> "The feet were indeed the one part iron, the other part clay, until the stone was cut out without hands, and struck the image upon the iron and clay feet, and dashed them into pieces, even to the end."
> (Daniel 2:33–34)

Then afterwards, when interpreting this, he says:

> "And as thou sawest the feet and the toes, partly indeed of clay, and partly of iron, the kingdom shall be divided, and there shall be in it a root of iron, as thou sawest iron mixed with baked clay. And the toes were indeed the one part iron, but the other part clay."
> (Daniel 2:41–42a)

---

[40]He is alluding to Revelation 17:11. This allusion further strengthens the link between the ten horns of the beast mentioned in Revelation 17 with the ten horns on the beast in Daniel 7.

[41]This is an allusion to Revelation 17:13. Now there should be no doubt that Revelation 17 and 18 describe events that take place as a consequence of the Jews accepting the AntiChrist as their Messiah.

[42]Here Irenæus has said it plainly. The "saints" put to flight are "the Church." By that he can only *mean* those who reject the AntiChrist.

The ten toes, therefore, are these ten kings, among whom the kingdom shall be partitioned, of whom some indeed shall be strong and active, or energetic; others, again, shall be sluggish and useless, and shall not agree; as also Daniel says:

> "Some part of the kingdom shall be strong, and part shall be broken from it. As thou sawest the iron mixed with the baked clay, there shall be minglings among the human race, but no cohesion one with the other, just as iron cannot be welded on to pottery ware." (Daniel 2:42b–43)

And since an end shall take place, he says:

> "And in the days of these kings shall the God of heaven raise up a kingdom which shall never decay, and His kingdom shall not be left to another people. It shall break in pieces and shatter all kingdoms, and shall itself be exalted for ever. As thou sawest that the stone was cut without hands from the mountain, and broke in pieces the baked clay, the iron, the brass, the silver, and the gold, God has pointed out to the king what shall come to pass after these things; and the dream is true, and the interpretation trustworthy." (Daniel 2:44–45)

2. If therefore the great God showed future things by Daniel, and confirmed them by His Son; and if Christ is the stone which is cut out without hands, who shall destroy temporal kingdoms, and introduce an eternal one, which is the resurrection of the just;[43] as he declares, "The God of heaven shall raise up a kingdom which shall never be destroyed,"—let those thus confuted come to their senses, who reject the Creator, and do not agree that the prophets were sent beforehand from the same Father from whom also the Lord came, but who assert that prophecies originated from diverse powers.

* * * * * *

CHAPTER XXIX

1. In the previous books I have set forth the causes for which God permitted these things to be made, and have pointed out that

---

[43]Note what he has said. "The resurrection of the just" will establish the eternal kingdom of God. Notice, however, the resurrection of the just occurs at the end of the reign of the AntiChrist.

all such have been created for the benefit of that human nature which is saved, ripening for immortality that which is [possessed] of its own free will and its own power, and preparing and rendering it more adapted for eternal subjection to God. And therefore the creation is suited to [the wants of] man; for man was not made for its sake, but creation for the sake of man.

Those nations, however, who did not of themselves raise up their eyes unto heaven, nor returned thanks to their Maker, nor wished to behold the light of truth, but who were like blind mice concealed in the depths of ignorance, the word justly reckons "as waste water from a sink, and as the turning–weight of a balance—in fact, as nothing;"[44] so far useful and serviceable to the just, as stubble conduces towards the growth of the wheat, and its straw, by means of combustion, serves for working gold. And therefore, when in the end the Church shall be suddenly caught up from this, it is said,

> "There shall be tribulation such as has not been since the beginning, neither shall be."
> (Daniel 12:1; Matthew 24:21)

For this is the last contest[45] of the righteous, in which, when they overcome, they are crowned with incorruption.

2. And there is therefore in this beast, when he comes, a recapitulation made of all sorts of iniquity and of every deceit, in order that all apostate power, flowing into and being shut up in him, may be sent into the furnace of fire. Fittingly, therefore, shall his name possess the number six hundred and sixty-six, since he sums up in his own person all the commixture of wickedness which took place previous to the deluge, due to the apostasy of the angels.[46] For Noah was six hundred years old when the deluge came upon the earth, sweeping away the rebellious world, for the sake of that most infa-

---

[44]Isaiah 40:15.

[45]Our time has been selected for yet another pitting of *The Light* of unadulterated Truth against the "darkness" of absolute ignorance. Scoffers will mock that statement, never considering for a moment that it might be true. True Believers take heed and prepare yourselves well now for that "contest." Your faith (belief in the Truth) will be all that will sustain you.

[46]Irenæus starts getting a little speculative here. Bear with him. He won't take long.

mous generation which lived in the times of Noah. And [Antichrist] also sums up every error of devised idols since the flood, together with the slaying of the prophets and the cutting off of the just. For that image which was set up by Nebuchadnezzar had indeed a height of sixty cubits, while the breadth was six cubits; on account of which Ananias, Azarias, and Misaël, when they did not worship it, were cast into a furnace of fire, pointing out prophetically, by what happened to them, the wrath against the righteous which shall arise towards the [time of the] end.

For that image, taken as a whole, was a prefiguring of this man's coming, decreeing that he should undoubtedly himself alone be worshipped by all men. Thus, then, the six hundred years of Noah, in whose time the deluge occurred because of the apostasy, and the number of the cubits of the image for which these just men were sent into the fiery furnace, do indicate the number of the name of that man in whom is concentrated the whole apostasy of six thousand years, and unrighteousness, and wickedness, and false prophecy, and deception; for which things sake a cataclysm of fire shall also come [upon the earth].[47]

CHAPTER XXX

1. Such, then, being the state of the case, and this number being found in all the most approved and ancient copies [of the Apocalypse], and *those men who saw John face to face bearing their testimony [to it]*;[48] while reason also leads us to conclude that the number of the name of the beast, [if reckoned] according to the Greek mode of calculation by the [value of] the letters contained in it, will amount to six hundred and sixty and six; that is, the number of tens shall be equal to that of the hundreds, and the number of hun-

---

[47]He is speaking of the events described in Revelation 17–18. He has alluded to the fire several times earlier.

[48]Wouldn't you love to have been even this close to hearing the words of Jesus Himself? Irenæus must have had opportunity to talk to several men who actually heard the Apostles teach. Yet many of his contemporaries with access to the same information were eagerly spouting their own opinions ("doing theology" as it were) while Irenæus attempted to faithfully pass on to his disciples—including—Hippolytus, *The Teaching* as he had *received* it from the Apostolic Fathers.

dreds equal to that of the units (for that number which [expresses] the digit six being adhered to throughout, indicates the recapitulations of that apostasy, taken in its full extent, which occurred at the beginning, during the intermediate periods, and which shall take place at the end).

I do not know how it is that some have erred following the ordinary mode of speech, and have vitiated the middle number in the name, deducting the amount of fifty from it, so that instead of six decads they will have it that there is but one. [I am inclined to think that this occurred through the fault of the copyists, as is wont to happen, since numbers also are expressed by letters; so that the Greek letter which expresses the number sixty was easily expanded into the letter Iota of the Greeks.][49]

Others then received this reading without examination; some in their simplicity, and upon their own responsibility, making use of this number expressing one decad; while some, in their inexperience, have ventured to seek out a name which should contain the erroneous and spurious number. Now, as regards those who have done this in simplicity, and without evil intent, we are at liberty to assume that pardon will be granted them by God. But as for those who, for the sake of vainglory, lay it down for certain that names containing the spurious number are to be accepted, and affirm that this name, hit upon by themselves, is that of him who is to come; such persons shall not come forth without loss, because they have led into error both themselves and those who confided in them.

Now, in the first place, *it is loss to wander from the truth, and to imagine that as being the case which is not;*[50] then again, as there shall be no light punishment [inflicted] upon him who either adds or subtracts anything from the Scripture,[51] under that such a person must necessarily fall. Moreover, another danger, by no means trifling, shall overtake those who falsely presume that they know the

---

[49]The words in brackets have been considered by some to be an interpolation.

[50]Note Irenæus' absolute confidence that there is but one true *meaning* to the Scriptures. He is also concerned about a lack of understanding regarding what most today would consider a trivial issue. How do you suppose he would react upon finding that the Church eventually distorted even the basic doctrine of salvation by faith?

[51]Revelation 22:18–19.

name of Antichrist.[52] For if these men assume one [number], when this [Antichrist] shall come having another, they will be easily led away by him, as supposing him not to be the expected one, who must be guarded against.

2. These men, therefore, ought to learn [what really is the state of the case], and go back to the true number of the name, that they be not reckoned among false prophets. But, knowing the sure number declared by Scripture, that is, six hundred sixty and six, let them await, in the first place, the division of the kingdom into ten; then, in the next place, when these kings are reigning, and beginning to set their affairs in order, and advance their kingdom, [let them learn] to acknowledge that *he who shall come claiming the kingdom*[53] *for himself, and shall terrify those men of whom we have been speaking,*[54] *having a name containing the aforesaid number, is truly the abomination of desolation. This, too, the apostle affirms:*

> "When they shall say, Peace and safety, then sudden destruction shall come upon them."
> (1 Thessalonians 5:3)

And Jeremiah does not merely point out his sudden coming,[55] but he even indicates the tribe from which he shall come, where he says,

> "We shall hear the voice of his swift horses from Dan; the whole earth shall be moved by the voice of the neighing of his galloping horses: he shall also come and devour the earth, and the fulness thereof, the city also, and they that dwell therein."
> (Jeremiah 8:16)

This, too, is the reason that this tribe is not reckoned in the Apocalypse along with those which are saved.[56]

---

[52]He clearly understands the number of the beast—666—reveals the name of the AntiChrist. But heed what he says. Those who "falsely presume that they know the name of Antichrist" stand in danger.

[53]He *means* the "Kingdom of God," that is, the kingdom of Israel on Earth.

[54]Notice the AntiChrist will subjugate the remaining seven rulers (out of the ten) by instilling fear.

[55]Irenæus understood the "sudden" destruction Paul was referring to is the appearance of the AntiChrist. It will be sudden. There will be no time for preparation then.

[56]Revelation 7:5–8.

3. It is therefore more certain, and less hazardous, to await the fulfillment of the prophecy,[57] than to be making surmises, and casting about for any names that may present themselves, inasmuch as many names can be found possessing the number mentioned; and the same question will, after all, remain unsolved.[58] For if there are many names found possessing this number, it will be asked which among them shall the coming man bear. It is not through a want of names containing the number of that name that I say this, but on account of the fear of God, and zeal for the truth: for the name Evanthas (ΕΥΑΝΘΑΣ) contains the required number, but I make no allegation regarding it.[59]

* * * * * *

---

[57]Irenæus *means* the prophecy of the Prophet Daniel concerning the "abomination of desolation" (Dan. 12:11). Only when the AntiChrist takes his seat in the rebuilt temple and "sets himself forth as God" will anyone know to beware of him. As Jesus said (Matt. 24:15), however, that is the time for action.

[58]I trust this will be advice well taken. When the time comes, the number will merely serve as confirmation.

[59]In the section omitted here, Irenæus discusses other names that also disclose the number 666. However, he concludes his discussion with the statement,

> We will not, however, incur the risk of pronouncing positively as to the name of Antichrist; for if it were necessary that his name should be distinctly revealed in this present time, it would have been announced by him who beheld the apocalyptic vision.

HIPPOLYTUS:
Treatise on Christ and AntiChrist

1. As it was your desire, my beloved brother Theophilus,[60] to be thoroughly informed on those topics which I put summarily before you, I have thought it right to set these matters of inquiry clearly forth to your view, drawing largely from the Holy Scriptures themselves as from a holy fountain, in order that you may not only have the pleasure of hearing them on the testimony of men, but may also be able, by surveying them in the light of (divine) authority, to glorify God in all. For this will be as a sure supply furnished you by us for your journey in this present life, so that by ready argument applying *things ill understood and apprehended by most*,[61] you may sow them in the ground of your heart, as in a rich and clean soil.

---

[60]Hippolytus seems to have written this work for an individual whom he considered to be his disciple. He discloses in the introductory paragraphs that he intends the recipient, Theophilus, to use the information to educate his own disciples in *The Teaching*. This mind-set is alien to the modern Church. Today, Believers are converted and then left to flounder, seeking someone—anyone—who can teach them the Truth and finding only confusion. Ultimately, most discover that the multiplicity of "right" doctrines provides a perfect cover for them to go their own way and do their own thing. Little do they realize God has used the confusing array of doctrines they so dearly love to test the hearts of men. They have been, as it were, tried in the balance and found wanting (Dan. 5:27).
[61]Hippolytus has just disclosed that "most" (in the Church) in his day did not "understand" or "apprehend" the things he has written here. The same applies to "most" in the Church today. The wise will pay attention to what Hippolytus fully understood.

By these, too, you will be able to silence those who oppose and gainsay the word of salvation. *Only see that you do not give these things over to unbelieving and blasphemous tongues, for that is no common danger.* But impart them to pious and faithful men, who desire to live holily and righteously with fear. For it is not to no purpose that the blessed apostle exhorts Timothy, and says,

> "O Timothy, keep that which is committed to thy trust, avoiding profane and vain babblings, and oppositions of science falsely so called; which some professing have erred concerning the faith." (1 Timothy 6:20, 21)

And again,[62]

> "Thou therefore, my son, be strong in the grace that is in Christ Jesus. And the things that thou hast heard of me in many exhorta-

---

[62]Here Hippolytus reveals that his Teacher(s) have taught him well, and that he has been an apt disciple. By reiterating Paul's words to Timothy he is emphasizing to his own disciple Theophilus that the role of the True Believer is to learn *The Teaching* as it is taught by *one who has been taught*. Likewise, the obligation of those whom God has called to be Teachers is to convey *The Teaching* to others just as they have been taught—changing nothing.

Unfortunately, early on the Church fell prey to false teachers, those whom God had not called to be Teachers, those who were unwilling to submit themselves to God and learn the Truth of *The Teaching* from others. These individuals spoke from the folly of their own mind to bolster their own ego. "I think . . ." and "It seems to me . . ." soon replaced "The apostles taught . . ." and "As Polycarp said . . ." Consequently, from the time of Origen (ca. A.D. 200) until now, the only "truth" available to the Church has been the speculative theology that arose when Church leaders foolishly blended *The Apostolic Teaching* with Greek philosophical concepts, creating a basic Systematic Theology.

In such speculative theology, there remained little room for the *parabolic imagery* and Hebrew idioms of the Old Testament Gospel. Hence, *The Teaching* the Apostles knew and taught was soon lost. All that remained of what the Apostles understood was the few written works we find in the New Testament. Even those contain *the mystery* sometimes couched in difficult-to-understand *parabolic statements*. (See *The Mystery of Scripture* and *The Way, The Truth, The Life* for a more complete discussion of how the Early Church lost *The Teaching*. See also "The Protestant Confession: The Church Lost *The Teaching*" in *The Voice of Elijah*, January 1992.)

tions, the same commit thou to faithful men, who shall be able to teach others also."
(2 Timothy 2:1, 2)

If, then, the blessed (apostle) delivered these things with a pious caution, which could be easily known by all, as he perceived in the spirit that "all men have not faith,"[63] *how much greater will be our danger, if, rashly and without thought, we commit the revelations of God to profane and unworthy men?*

2. For as the blessed prophets were made, so to speak, eyes for us, *they foresaw through faith the mysteries of the word*, and became ministers of these things also to succeeding generations, not only reporting the past, but also announcing the present and the future, so that the prophet might not appear to be one only for the time being, but might also predict the future for all generations, and so be reckoned a (true) prophet. For these fathers were furnished with the Spirit, and largely honoured by the Word Himself; and just as it is with instruments of music, so had they the Word always, like the plectrum[64] in union with them and when moved by Him the prophets announced what God willed.

For they spake not of their own power[65] (let there be no mistake as to that) neither did they declare what pleased themselves. But first of all they were endowed with wisdom by the Word, and then again were rightly instructed in the future by means of visions.[66] And then, when thus themselves fully convinced, *they spake those things which were revealed by God to them alone, and concealed from all others*. For with what reason should the prophet be called a prophet, unless he in spirit foresaw the future?

For if the prophet spake of any chance event, he would not be a prophet then in speaking of things which were under the eye of all. But one who sets forth in detail things yet to be, was rightly judged a prophet. Wherefore prophets were with good reason called from the very first "seers."[67]

---

[63] 2 Thessalonians 3:2.
[64] The plectrum was a piece of ivory or metal, much like a guitar pick, which was used in playing the lyre.
[65] 2 Peter 1:21.
[66] Numbers 12:6–8.
[67] 1 Samuel 9:9.

And hence we, too, who are rightly instructed in what was declared aforetime by them, speak not of our own capacity. For we do not attempt to make any change one way or another among ourselves in the words that were spoken of old by them, but we make the Scriptures in which these are written public, and read them to those who can believe rightly; for that is a common benefit for both parties: for him who speaks, in holding in memory and setting forth correctly things uttered of old;[68] and for him who hears, in giving attention to the things spoken.

* * * * * *

5. But as time now presses for the consideration of the question immediately in hand, and as what has been already said in the intro-

---

[68]Hippolytus clearly understood he had been *"rightly instructed in what was declared aforetime by them"* (the Prophets). He also knew that an accurate understanding of the Gospel could only come by having been "rightly instructed." In turn, he believed the ministry of Teachers (those "who are rightly instructed") was to ensure that no change was made in *The Apostolic Teaching* they had *received*. They were expected to "hold it in memory" and "set it forth correctly." Of all the Early Church Fathers, Hippolytus and his Teacher, Irenæus, seem to have been most faithful to God's plan in which the Teachers of the Church were to be the repository and transmitters of *The Teaching* to subsequent generations. (See "Where Are Jesus' Disciples?" in *The Voice of Elijah*, April 1991.)

Others in the time of Irenæus and Hippolytus were not as faithful as these two men were, however. Origen, a contemporary of Hippolytus, openly propounded allegorical interpretation as a legitimate means whereby thieves and robbers "could climb up some other way" (John 10:1). He taught that Church leaders should interpret the Scriptures for themselves. During that same period of time, Hippolytus was waging a losing battle with secularism. He managed to convict two of the bishops in Rome of heresy and living in open sin; yet he lost the battle for doctrinal purity to Origen's oratory and prolific writing. Consequently, by A.D. 250, the Orthodox Church was already well on its way toward total blindness as to the Truth of *The Teaching*. Although the fundamental truth of the Gospel message remained in the Church, the rest of *The Teaching* was eventually lost. From the time of Hippolytus, however, there remained yet thirteen centuries of uninhibited dalliance with the world before Martin Luther and John Calvin came to *restore* just the basics of the Truth of the Gospel message.

duction with regard to the glory of God, may suffice, it is proper that we take the Holy Scriptures themselves in hand, and find out from them:[69]

1) what, and of what manner, the coming of Antichrist is;

2) on what occasion and at what time that impious one shall be revealed; and

3) whence and from what tribe (he shall come); and

4) what his name is, which is indicated by the number in the Scripture; and

5) how he shall work error among the people, gathering them from the ends of the earth; and

6) (how) he shall stir up tribulation and persecution against the saints; and

7) how he shall glorify himself as God; and

8) what his end shall be; and

9) how the sudden appearing of the Lord shall be revealed from heaven; and

10) what the conflagration of the whole world shall be; and

11) what the glorious and heavenly kingdom of the saints is to be, when they reign together with Christ; and

12) what the punishment of the wicked by fire.

6. Now, as our Lord Jesus Christ, who is also God, was prophesied of under the figure of a lion,[70] on account of His royalty and glory, in the same way have the Scriptures also aforetime spoken of Antichrist as a lion, on account of his tyranny and violence. For the deceiver seeks to liken himself in all things to the Son of God.[71]

---

[69]What follows is an outline of what Hippolytus intends to explain for his disciple Theophilus in the following pages.

[70]Revelation 5:5.

[71]This is the clearest statement Hippolytus makes in this work concerning Satan's motives in becoming incarnate as the AntiChrist. He "seeks to liken himself to the Son of God," that is, by pretending to be Jesus Christ, the legitimate Messiah of Israel, and seeking to be recognized as such. Hippolytus now gives a detailed list of how Satan emulates Jesus Christ.

1) Christ is a lion, so Antichrist is also a lion;

2) Christ is a king,[72] so Antichrist is also a king.

3) The Saviour was manifested as a lamb;[73] so he too, in like manner, will appear as a lamb, though within he is a wolf. [74]

4) The Saviour came into the world in the circumcision, and he will come in the same manner.

5) The Lord sent apostles among all the nations, and he in like manner will send false apostles.

6) The Saviour gathered together the sheep that were scattered abroad,[75] and he in like manner will bring together a people that is scattered abroad.

7) The Lord gave a seal to those who believed on Him, and he will give one in like manner.

8) The Saviour appeared in the form of man, and he too will come in the form of a man.

9) The Saviour raised up and showed His holy flesh like a temple, and *he will raise a temple of stone in Jerusalem.*

And his seductive arts we shall exhibit in what follows. But for the present let us turn to the question in hand.

* * * * * *

19. These words then being thus presented, let us observe somewhat in detail what Daniel says in his visions. For in distinguishing the kingdoms that are to rise after these things, he showed also the coming of Antichrist in the last times, and THE CONSUMMATION OF THE WHOLE WORLD. In expounding the vision of Nebuchadnezzar, then, he speaks thus:

---

[72] John 18:37.

[73] John 1:29.

[74] The qualities of gentleness and meekness are those the AntiChrist will first present to the world. Yet when he has been accepted as the messianic king of Israel in the middle of the final week, he will manifest himself as a wolf, as Hippolytus says, "on account of his tyranny and violence."

[75] John 11:52.

"Thou O king, sawest, and behold a great image standing before thy face: the head of which was of fine gold, its arms and shoulders of silver, its belly and its thighs of brass, and its legs of iron, (and) its feet part of iron and part of clay. Thou sawest, then, till that a stone was cut out without hands, and smote the image upon the feet that were of iron and clay, and brake them to an end. Then were the clay, the iron, the brass, the silver, (and) the gold broken, and became like the chaff from the summer threshing-floor; and the strength (fulness) of the wind carried them away, and there was no place found for them. And the stone that smote the image became a great mountain, and filled the whole earth."
(Daniel 2:31–35)

20. Now if we set Daniel's own visions also side by side with this, we shall have one exposition to give of the two together, and shall (be able to) show how concordant with each other they are, and how true. For he speaks thus:

"I Daniel saw, and behold the four winds of the heaven strove upon the great sea. And four great beasts came up from the sea, diverse one from another. The first (was) like a lioness, and had wings as of an eagle. I beheld till the wings thereof were plucked, and it was lifted up from the earth and made stand upon the feet as a man, and a man's heart was given to it. And behold a second beast like to a bear, and it was made stand on one part, and it had three ribs in the mouth of it. I beheld, and lo a beast like a leopard, and it had upon the back of it four wings of a fowl, and the beast had four heads. After this I saw, and behold a fourth beast, dreadful and terrible, and strong exceedingly; it had iron teeth *and claws of brass*, which devoured and brake in pieces, and it stamped the residue with the feet of it; and it was diverse from all the beasts that were before it, and it had ten horns. I considered its horns, and behold there came up among them another little horn, and before it there were three of the first horns plucked up by the roots; and behold in this horn were eyes like the eyes of man, and a mouth speaking great things. (21.) I beheld till the thrones were set, and the Ancient of days did sit: and His garment was white as snow, and the hair of His head; like pure wool: His throne was a flame of fire, His wheels were a burning fire. A stream of fire flowed before Him. Thousand thousands ministered unto Him: and ten thousand times ten thousand stood around Him: the judgement was set, and the books were Opened. I beheld then, because of the voice of the great words which the horn spake, till the beast was slain and perished, and his body given to the burning of fire. And

the dominion of the other beasts was taken away. (22.) I saw in the night vision, and, behold, one like the Son of man was coming with the clouds of heaven, and came to the Ancient of days, and was brought near before Him. And there was given Him dominion, and honour, and the kingdom; and all peoples, tribes, and tongues shall serve Him: His dominion is an everlasting dominion, which shall not pass away, and His kingdom shall not be destroyed."
(Daniel 7:2–14)

23. Now since these things, spoken as they are with a mystical meaning, may seem to some hard to understand, we shall keep back nothing fitted to impart an intelligent apprehension of them to those who are possessed of a sound mind. He said, then, that a "lioness came up from the sea," and by that he meant the kingdom of the Babylonians in the world, which also was the head of gold on the image.

In saying that "it had wings as of an eagle," he meant that Nebuchadnezzar the king was lifted up and was exalted against God. Then he says, "the wings thereof were plucked," that is to say, his glory was destroyed; for he was driven out of his kingdom. And the words, "a man's heart was given to it, and it was made stand upon the feet as a man," refer to the fact that he repented and recognised himself to be only a man, and gave the glory to God.

24. Then, after the lioness, he sees a "second beast like a bear," and that denoted the Persians. For after the Babylonians, the Persians held the sovereign power. And in saying that there were "three ribs in the mouth of it," he pointed to three nations, viz., the Persians, and the Medes, and the Babylonians; which were also represented on the image by the silver after the gold. Then (there was) "the third beast, a leopard," which meant the Greeks. For after the Persians, Alexander of Macedon obtained the sovereign power on subverting Darius, as is also shown by the brass on the image. And in saying that it had "four wings of a fowl," he taught us most clearly how the kingdom of Alexander was partitioned. For in speaking of "four heads," he made mention of four kings, viz., those who arose out of that (kingdom). For Alexander, when dying, partitioned out his kingdom into four divisions.

25. Then he says: "A fourth beast, dreadful and terrible; it had iron teeth and claws of brass." And who are these but the Romans? which (kingdom) is meant by the iron —the kingdom which is now

established; for the legs of that (image) were of iron. And after this, what remains, beloved, but the toes of the feet of the image, in which part is iron and part clay, mixed together?

And mystically by the toes of the feet he meant the kings who are to arise from among them; as Daniel also says (in the words),

> "I considered the beast, and lo there were ten horns behind it, among which shall rise another (horn), an offshoot, and shall pluck up by the roots the three (that were) before it."
> (Daniel 7:8)

And under this was signified none other than *Antichrist, who is also himself to raise the kingdom of the Jews*.[76] He says that three horns are plucked up by the root by him, viz., the three kings of Egypt, and Libya, and Ethiopia,[77] whom he cuts off in the array of battle. And he, after gaining terrible power over all, being nevertheless a tyrant, shall stir up tribulation and persecution against men, exalting himself against them. For Daniel says:

> "I considered the horn, and behold that horn made war with the saints, and prevailed against them, till the beast was slain and perished, and its body was given to the burning of fire."
> (Daniel 7:21, 11)

26. After a little space the stone[78] will come from heaven which smites the image and breaks it in pieces, and subverts all the kingdoms, and gives the kingdom to the saints of the Most High. This is the stone which becomes a great mountain, and fills the whole earth, of which Daniel says:

> "I saw in the night visions, and behold one like the Son of man came with the clouds of heaven, and came to the Ancient of days, and was brought near before Him. And there was given Him dominion, and glory, and a kingdom; and all peoples, tribes, and

---

[76]He says "kingdom," not "nation." The "nation" of the Jews exists now, but will not become a "kingdom" until the Jews recognize their messiah and anoint him as king. However you should beware. The Jews could easily establish the "office" of messiah first. That office could be occupied by a succession of individuals before the AntiChrist finally succeeds in rebuilding the temple, then takes his seat there, representing himself as God and thereby becoming the "abomination of desolation."

[77]He has obtained this information from Daniel 11:43.

[78]Daniel 2:34–35.

languages shall serve Him: and His dominion is an everlasting dominion, which shall not pass away, and His kingdom shall not be destroyed."
(Daniel 7:13–14)

He showed all power given by the Father to the Son,[79] who is ordained Lord of things in heaven, and things on earth, and things under the earth, and Judge of all:[80] of things in heaven, because He was born, the Word of God, before all (ages); and of things on earth, because He became man in the midst of men, to re-create our Adam through Himself; and of things under the earth, because He was also reckoned among the dead, preaching the Gospel to the souls of the saints,[81] (and) by death overcoming death.

27. As these things, then, are in the future, and as the ten toes of the image are equivalent to (so many) democracies, and the ten horns of the fourth beast are distributed over ten kingdoms, let us look at the subject a little more closely, and consider these matters as in the clear light of a personal survey.

28. The golden head of the image and the lioness denoted the Babylonians; the shoulders and arms of silver, and the bear, represented the Persians and Medes; the belly and thighs of brass, and the leopard, meant the Greeks, who held the sovereignty from Alexander's time; the legs of iron, and the beast dreadful and terrible, expressed the Romans, who hold the sovereignty at present; the toes of the feet which were part clay and part iron, and the ten horns, were emblems of the kingdoms that are yet to rise; the other little horn that grows up among them meant the Antichrist in their midst; the stone that smites the earth and brings judgment upon the world was Christ.

29. *These things, beloved, we impart to you with fear, and yet readily, on account of the love of Christ, which surpasseth all. For if the blessed prophets who preceded us did not choose to proclaim these things, though they knew them, openly and boldly, lest they should disquiet the souls of men, but recounted them mystically in parables and dark sayings, speaking thus, "Here is the mind which hath wisdom,"[82] how much greater risk shall we run in venturing to declare*

---

[79]Matthew 28:18.
[80]Philippians 2:10.
[81]1 Peter 3:19.
[82]Revelation 17:9.

openly things spoken by them in obscure terms![83] Let us look, therefore, at the things which are to befall this unclean harlot in the last days; and (let us consider) what and what manner of tribulation is destined to visit her in the wrath of God before the judgment as an earnest of her doom.

30. Come, then, O blessed Isaiah; arise, tell us clearly what thou didst prophesy with respect to the mighty Babylon. For thou didst speak also of Jerusalem, and thy word is accomplished. For thou didst speak boldly and openly:

> "Your country is desolate, your cities are burned with fire; your land, strangers devour it in your presence, and it is desolate as overthrown by many strangers. The daughter of Sion shall be left as a cottage in a vineyard, and as a lodge in a garden of cucumbers, as a besieged city."
> (Isaiah 1:7–8)

What then? Are not these things come to pass? Are not the things announced by thee fulfilled? Is not their country, Judea, desolate? Is not the holy place burned with fire? Are not their walls cast down? Are not their cities destroyed? Their land, do not strangers devour it? Do not the Romans rule the country? And indeed these impious people hated thee, and did saw thee asunder, and they crucified Christ. Thou art dead in the world, but thou livest in Christ.

31. Which of you, then, shall I esteem more than thee? Yet Jeremiah, too, is stoned. But if I should esteem Jeremiah most, yet Daniel too has his testimony. Daniel, I commend thee above all; yet John too gives no false witness. With how many mouths and tongues would I praise you; or rather the Word who spake in you! Ye died with Christ; and ye will live with Christ. Hear ye, and rejoice; behold the things announced by you have been fulfilled in their time. For ye saw these things yourselves first, and then ye proclaimed them to all generations.

---

[83]Here Hippolytus expresses a clear reticence to speak concerning the true *meaning* of things that he understood about the *parabolic imagery* of the Old Testament message. The fact that he immediately launches into the matter of this present world being represented as *Mystery Babylon*, the harlot, discloses he understood the larger part, if not all, of the Book of Revelation. I have explained this imagery somewhat in "Is Iraq Mystery Babylon?" in *The Voice of Elijah*, January 1991.

Ye ministered the oracles of God to all generations. Ye prophets were called, that ye might be able to save all. For then is one a prophet indeed, when, having announced beforetime things about to be, he can afterwards show that they have actually happened. Ye were the disciples of a good Master. These words I address to you as if alive, and with propriety. For ye hold already the crown of life and immortality which is laid up for you in heaven.[84]

32. Speak with me, O blessed Daniel. Give me full assurance, I beseech thee. Thou dost prophesy concerning the lioness in Babylon;[85] for thou wast a captive there. Thou hast unfolded the future regarding the bear; for thou wast still in the world, and didst see the things come to pass. Then thou speakest to me of the leopard; and whence canst thou know this, for thou art already gone to thy rest? Who instructed thee to announce these things, but He who formed thee in (from) thy mother's womb?[86] That is God, thou sayest. Thou hast spoken indeed, and that not falsely. The leopard has arisen; the he-goat is come; he hath smitten the ram; he hath broken his horns in pieces; he hath stamped upon him with his feet. He has been exalted by his fall; (the) four horns have come up from under that one.[87] Rejoice, blessed Daniel! Thou hast not been in error: all these things have come to pass.

33. After this again thou hast told me of the beast dreadful and terrible.

"It had iron teeth and claws of brass: it devoured and brake in pieces, and stamped the residue with the feet of it."
(Daniel 7:7)

Already the iron rules; already it subdues and breaks all in pieces; already it brings all the unwilling into subjection; already we see these things ourselves. Now we glorify God, being instructed by thee.

34. But as the task before us was to speak of the harlot, be thou with us, O blessed Isaiah. Let us mark what thou sayest about Babylon.

---

[84]2 Timothy 4:8.
[85]Daniel 7:4.
[86]Jeremiah 1:5.
[87]Daniel 8:2–8.

"Come down, sit upon the ground, O virgin daughter of Babylon; sit, O daughter of the Chaldeans; thou shalt no longer be called tender and delicate. Take the millstone, grind meal, draw aside thy veil, shave the grey hairs, make bare the legs, pass over the rivers. Thy shame shall be uncovered, thy reproach shall be seen: I will take justice of thee, I will no more give thee over to men. As for thy Redeemer, (He is) the Lord of hosts, the Holy One of Israel is his name. Sit thou in compunction, get thee into darkness, O daughter of the Chaldeans: thou shalt no longer be called the strength of the kingdom. (35.) I was wroth with my people; I have polluted mine inheritance, I have given them into thine hand: and thou didst show them no mercy; but upon the ancient (the elders) thou hast very heavily laid thy yoke. And thou saidst, I shall be a princess for ever: thou didst not lay these things to thy heart, neither didst remember thy latter end. Therefore hear now this, thou that art delicate; that sittest, that art confident, that sayest in thine heart, I am, and there is none else; I shall not sit as a widow, neither shall I know the loss of children. But, now these two things shall come upon thee in one day, widowhood and the loss of children: they shall come upon thee suddenly in thy sorcery, in the strength of thine enchantments mightily, in the hope of thy fornication. For thou hast said, I am, and there is none else. And thy fornication shall be thy shame, because thou hast said in thy heart, I am. And destruction shall come upon thee, and thou shalt not know it. *(And there shall be) a pit, and thou shall fall into it; and misery shall fall upon thee, and thou shalt not be able to be made clean; and destruction shall come upon thee, and thou shalt not know it.* Stand now with thy enchantments, and with the multitude of thy sorceries, which thou hast learned from thy youth; if so be thou shalt be able to be profited. Thou art wearied in thy counsels. Let the astrologers of the heavens stand and save thee; let the star-gazers announce to thee what shall come upon thee. Behold, they shall all be as sticks for the fire; so shall they be burned, and they shall not deliver their soul from the flame. Because thou hast coals of fire, sit upon them; so shall it be for thy help. Thou art wearied with change from thy youth. Man has gone astray (each one) by himself; and there shall be no salvation for thee."
(Isaiah 47:1–15)

These things does Isaiah prophesy for thee. Let us see now whether John has spoken to the same effect.

36. For he sees, when in the isle Patmos, a revelation of awful mysteries, which he recounts freely, and makes known to others. Tell

me, blessed John, apostle and disciple of the Lord, what didst thou see and hear concerning Babylon? Arise, and speak; for it sent thee also into banishment.[88]

"And there came one of the seven angels which had the seven vials, and talked with me, saying unto me, Come hither; I will show unto thee the judgment of the great whore that sitteth upon many waters; with whom the kings of the earth have committed fornication, and the inhabitants of the earth have been made drunk with the wine of her fornication. And he carried me away in the spirit into the wilderness: and I saw a woman sit upon a scarlet-coloured beast, full of names of blasphemy, having seven heads and ten horns. And the woman was arrayed in purple and scarlet colour, and decked with gold, and precious stone, and pearls, having a golden cup in her hand, full of abominations and filthiness of the fornication of the earth. Upon her forehead was a name written, Mystery, Babylon the Great, the Mother of Harlots and Abominations of the Earth.

37. And I saw the woman drunken with the blood of the saints, and with the blood of the martyrs of Jesus: and when I saw her, I wondered with great admiration. And the angel said unto me, Wherefore didst thou marvel? I will tell thee the mystery of the woman, and of the beast that carrieth her, which hath the seven heads and the ten horns. The beast that thou sawest was, and is not; and shall ascend out of the bottomless pit, and go into perdition: and they that dwell on the earth shall wonder (whose name was not written in the book of life from the foundation of the world) when they behold the beast that was, and is not, and yet shall be.

38. And here is the mind that has wisdom. The seven heads are seven mountains, on which the woman sitteth. And there are seven kings: five are fallen, and one is, and the other is not yet

---

[88]Having just quoted one of the most obvious Old Testament *parabolic statements* concerning this present civilization as the harlot Babylon (Is. 47:1–15), Hippolytus immediately turns to the vision John saw concerning the destruction of this realm at the end. His point will be lost on the one who fails to understand the parables of the Prophets. In those parables, *Mystery Babylon* is the civilization of this world. One could argue from the text that Hippolytus is referring to the Roman government that banished John to the Isle of Patmos. That overlooks entirely his understanding of the Old Testament *parabolic imagery.* He is referring to this world's government and the civilization under its dominion.

come; and when he cometh, he must continue a short space. And the beast that was *and* is not, (even he is the eighth) and is of the seven, and goeth into perdition. And the ten horns which thou sawest are ten kings, which have received no kingdom as yet; but receive power as kings one hour with the beast. These have one mind, and shall give their power and strength unto the beast. These shall make war with the Lamb, and the Lamb shall overcome them: for he is Lord of lords, and King of kings and they that are with Him are called, and chosen, and faithful.

39. And he saith to me, The waters which thou sawest, where the whore sitteth, are peoples, and multitudes, and nations, and tongues. And the ten horns which thou sawest, and the beast, these shall hate the whore, and shall make her desolate and naked, and shall eat her flesh, and burn her with fire. For God hath put in their hearts to fulfil His will, and to agree, and give their kingdom unto the beast, until the words of God shall be fulfilled. And the woman which thou sawest is that great city, which reigneth over the kings of the earth.

40. After these things I saw another angel come down from heaven, having great power; and the earth was lightened with his glory. And he cried mightily with a strong voice, saying, Babylon the great is fallen, is fallen, and is become the habitation of devils, and the hold of every foul spirit, *and a cage of every unclean* and hateful bird. For all nations have drunk of the wine of the wrath of her fornication, and the kings of the earth have committed fornication with her and the merchants of the earth are waxed rich through the abundance of her delicacies. And I heard another voice from heaven, saying, Come out of her, my people, that ye be not partakers of her sins, and that ye receive not of her plagues: for her sins did cleave even unto heaven, and God hath remembered her iniquities.

41. Reward her even as she rewarded (you), and double unto her double, according to her works: in the cup which she hath filled, fill to her double. How much she hath glorified herself, and lived deliciously, so much torment and sorrow give her: for she saith in her heart, I sit a queen, and am no widow, and shall see no sorrow. Therefore shall her plagues come in one day, death, and mourning, and famine; and she shall be utterly burned with fire: for strong is the Lord God who judgeth her. And the kings of the earth, who have committed fornication, and lived deliciously with her, shall bewail her, and lament for her, when they shall see the smoke of her burning, standing afar off for the fear of her torment, saying,

Alas, alas! that great city Babylon, that mighty city! for in one hour is thy judgment come. And the merchants of the earth shall weep and mourn over her; for no man shall buy their merchandise any more. The merchandise of gold, and silver, and precious stones, and of pearls, and fine linen, and purple, and silk, and scarlet, and all thyine wood, and all manner vessels of ivory, and all manner vessels of most precious wood, and of brass, and iron, and marble, and cinnamon, and spices, and odours, and ointments, and frankincense, and wine, and oil, and fine flour, and wheat, and beasts, and sheep, and goats, and horses, and chariots, and slaves (bodies), and souls of men. And the fruits that thy soul lusted after are departed from thee, and all things which were dainty and goodly have perished from thee, and thou shalt find them no more at all. The merchants of these things, which were made rich by her, shall stand afar off for the fear of her torment, weeping and wailing, and saying, Alas, alas! that great city, that was clothed in fine linen, and purple, and scarlet, and decked with gold, and precious stones, and pearls! for in one hour so great riches is come to nought. And every shipmaster, and all the company in ships, and sailors, and as many as trade by sea, stood afar off, and cried, when they saw the smoke of her burning, saying, what city is like unto this great city? And they cast dust on their heads, and cried, weeping and wailing, saying, Alas, alas! that great city, wherein were made rich all that had ships in the sea by reason of her fatness! for in one hour is she made desolate.

42. Rejoice over her, thou heaven, and ye angels, and apostles, and prophets; for God hath avenged you on her. And a mighty angel took up a stone like a great millstone, and cast it into the sea, saying, Thus with violence shall that great city Babylon be thrown down, and shall be found no more at all. And the voice of harpers and musicians, and of pipers and trumpeters, shall be heard no more at all in thee; and no craftsman, of whatsoever craft he be, shall be found any more in thee; and the sound of a millstone shall be heard no more at all in thee; and the light of a candle shall shine no more at all in thee and the voice of the bridegroom and of the bride shall be heard no more at all in thee: for thy merchants were the great men of the earth; for by thy sorceries were all nations deceived. And in her was found the blood of prophets and of saints, and of all that were slain upon the earth."
(Revelation 17:1–18:24)

43. With respect, then, to the particular judgment in *the torments that are to come upon it in the last times by the hand of the*

tyrants who shall arise then,[89] *the clearest statement has been given in these passages.*[90] But it becomes us further diligently to examine and set forth the period at which these things shall come to pass, and how the little horn shall spring up in their midst. For *when the legs of iron have issued in the feet and toes*, according to the similitude of the image and that of the terrible beast, as has been shown in the above, (then shall be the time) when the iron and the clay shall be mingled together. Now Daniel will set forth this subject to us. For he says,

> "And one week will make a covenant with many, and it shall be that in the midst (half) of the week my sacrifice and oblation shall cease."
> (Daniel 9:27)

By one week, therefore, *he meant the last week which is to be at the end of the whole world;*[91] of which week the two prophets Enoch and Elijah[92] will take up the half. For they will preach 1,260 days clothed in sackcloth, proclaiming repentance to the people and to all the nations.

44. For as two advents of our Lord and Savior are indicated in the Scriptures, the one being His first advent in the flesh, which took

---

[89]By "the tyrants," Hippolytus seems to *mean* the seven remaining rulers of the ten rulers represented by the ten horns and ten toes of Daniel's visions. They and the AntiChrist will be responsible for the final conflagration that destroys this realm.

[90]What a statement! How can he possibly think that these passages from Isaiah and Revelation contain "the clearest statement?" No other part of the Scriptures could possibly have such a diversity of opinion regarding its *meaning* as has the Book of Revelation! Yet when *The Teaching* is fully understood, Hippolytus' statement will be found to be true, confirming again just how much he knew of the apostolic tradition.

[91]Here he states clearly that the end of this civilization as we now know it will occur at the conclusion of the reign of the AntiChrist.

[92]The Early Church assumed that because one of the two witnesses would be ministering according to the *parabolic imagery* of Elijah as John the Baptist did, the other witness must be Enoch, since Enoch and Elijah are both mentioned in the Old Testament as having been taken into heaven alive (Gen. 5:24; 2 Kings 2:1 ff.). Notice that the ministry of these two witnesses spans the first half of the week, until the AntiChrist is anointed as the messianic king of Israel and has completed the building of the temple in Jerusalem. He will then have the two witnesses killed because of their testimony concerning his true nature.

place without honour by reason of His being set at nought, as Isaiah spake of Him aforetime, saying,

> "We saw Him, and He had no form nor comeliness, but His form was despised (and) rejected[93] above all men; a man smitten and familiar with bearing infirmity, (for His face was turned away); He was despised, and esteemed not."
> (Isaiah 53:2–3)

But His second advent is announced as glorious, when He shall come from heaven with the host of angels, and the glory of His Father, as the prophet saith, "Ye shall see the King in glory;"[94] and,

> "I saw one like the Son of man coming with the clouds of heaven; and he came to the Ancient of days, and he was brought to Him. And there were given Him dominion, and honour, and glory, and the kingdom; all tribes and languages shall serve Him: His dominion is an everlasting dominion, which shall not pass away."
> (Daniel 7:13–14)

Thus also *two forerunners*[95] were indicated. *The first was John the son of Zacharias*, who appeared in all things a forerunner and herald of our Saviour, preaching of the heavenly light that had appeared in the world. He first fulfilled the course of forerunner, and that from his mother's womb, being conceived by Elisabeth, in order that to those, too, who are children from their mother's womb he might declare the new birth that was to take place for their sakes by the Holy Ghost and the Virgin.

45. He, on hearing the salutation addressed to Elisabeth, leaped with joy in his mother's womb, recognising God the Word conceived in the womb of the Virgin. Thereafter he came forward

---

[93]Literally, "deficient."

[94]Isaiah 33:17.

[95]Of the two forerunners of Christ to whom Hippolytus has referred earlier, he mentions here only John the Baptist, the forerunner who proclaimed the first advent of Jesus Christ. He assumes the reader will understand by his earlier reference to Elijah that Elijah is the second forerunner of Jesus Christ, the one who announces His second advent. I wonder how "many" today actually believe those passages where Jesus said Elijah would come? That's a difficult one, isn't it? Even if you expected him, how would you know who he was? Jesus told you. You "shall know of *The Teaching*" (John 7:17).

preaching in the wilderness, proclaiming the baptism of repentance to the people, (and thus) announcing prophetically salvation to the nations living in the wilderness of the world. After this, at the Jordan, seeing the Saviour with his own eye, he points Him out, and says,

"Behold the Lamb of God, that taketh away the sin of the world!" (John 1:29)

He also first preached to those in Hades,[96] becoming a forerunner there when he was put to death by Herod, that there too he might intimate that the Saviour would descend to ransom the souls of the saints from the hand of death.

46. But since the Saviour was the beginning of the resurrection of all men, it was meet that the Lord alone should rise from the dead, by whom too the judgment is to enter for the whole world, that they who have wrestled worthily may be also crowned worthily by Him, by the illustrious Arbiter, to wit, who Himself first accomplished the course, and was received into the heavens, and was set down on the right hand of God the Father, and is to be manifested again at the end of the world as Judge.

It is a matter of course that His forerunners must appear first, as He says by Malachi, even the messenger:[97]

"I will send to you Elijah the Tishbite before the day of the Lord, the great and notable day, comes; and he shall turn the hearts of the fathers to the children, and the disobedient to the wisdom of the just, lest I come and smite the earth utterly." (Malachi 4:5–6)

These,[98] then, shall come and proclaim the manifestation of Christ that is to be from heaven; and they shall also perform signs and wonders, in order that men may be put to shame and turned to repentance for their surpassing wickedness and impiety.

---

[96] 1 Peter 3:18–19.

[97] I have substituted a secondary reading here. The translator was uncertain as to whether "even the messenger" should be translated "and the angel." "Even the messenger" is more relevant in context in as much as the Hebrew name Malachi *means* "my messenger." The difficulty arises because "angel" is just an English transliteration of the Greek term for "messenger" (*angelos*).

[98] By "these," Hippolytus *means* the two messengers he has earlier called Enoch and Elijah.

47. For John says,

> "And I will give power unto my two witnesses, and they shall prophesy a thousand two hundred and threescore days, clothed in sackcloth."
> (Revelation 11:3)

That is the half of the week whereof Daniel spake.[99]

> "These are the two olive trees and the two candlesticks standing before the Lord of the earth. And if any man will hurt them, fire will proceed out of their mouth, and devour their enemies; and if any man will hurt them, he must in this manner be killed. These have power to shut heaven, that it rain not in the days of their prophecy; and have power over waters, to turn them to blood, and to smite the earth with all plagues as often as *they will*. And when they shall have finished their course and their testimony."
> (Revelation 11:4–7a)

What saith the prophet?

> "The beast that ascendeth out of the bottomless pit shall make war against them, and shall overcome them, and kill them,"
> (Revelation 11:7b)

because they will not give glory to Antichrist. For this is meant by the little horn that grows up. He, being now elated in heart, begins to exalt himself, and to glorify himself as God, persecuting the saints and blaspheming Christ, even as Daniel says,

> "I considered the horn, and, behold, in the horn were eyes like the eyes of man, and a mouth speaking great things; and he opened his mouth to blaspheme God. And that horn made war against the saints, and prevailed against them until the beast was slain, and perished, and his body was given to be burned."
> (Daniel 7:8, 21, 11)

48. But as it is incumbent on us to discuss this matter of the beast more exactly, and in particular the question how the Holy Spirit has also mystically indicated his name by means of a number, we shall proceed to state more clearly what bears upon him. John then speaks thus:

---

[99]This statement seems enigmatic because Daniel speaks concerning the whole week, the middle of the week, and the last half of the week. Elsewhere, however, Hippolytus clearly states the two witnesses minister during the first half of the week by warning against the AntiChrist.

"And I beheld another beast coming up out of the earth; and he had two horns, like a lamb, and he spake as a dragon. And he exercised all the power of the first beast before him; and he made the earth and them which dwell therein to worship the first beast, whose deadly wound was healed. And he did great wonders, so that he maketh fire come down from heaven on the earth in the sight of men, and deceiveth them that dwell on the earth by means of those miracles which he had power to do in the sight of the beast, saying to them that dwell on the earth, that they should make an image to the beast which had the wound by a sword and did live. And he had power to give life unto the image of the beast, *that the image of the beast should both speak,* and cause that as many as would not worship the image of the beast should be killed. And he caused all, both small and great, rich and poor, free and bond, to receive a mark in their right hand or in their forehead; and that no man might buy or sell, save he that had the mark, the name of the beast, or the number of his name. Here is wisdom. Let him that hath understanding count the number of the beast; for it is the number of a man, and his number is six hundred threescore and six."
(Revelation 13:11–18)

49. By the beast, then, coming up out of the earth, he means the kingdom of Antichrist;[100] and by the two horns he means him and the false prophet after him.[101] And in speaking of "the horns being like a lamb," he means that *he will make himself like the Son of God,*

---

[100]The definition of "the beast" as a "kingdom," that is, as the kingdom of the AntiChrist, makes the vision of John correspond to, and contribute additional detail to, the visions of Daniel 7. In Daniel's vision, the kingdoms are all represented as "beasts" and all of the beasts come "out of the sea." Hippolytus explains below that the first beast mentioned in Revelation 13 is actually the fourth beast of Daniel 7, and that the second beast mentioned in Revelation 13 is a restoration of that kingdom. The first beast in Revelation 13, like the beasts in Daniel 7, comes "out of the sea." But the second beast of Revelation 13 (ominously) comes "out of the earth." The *parabolic imagery* of the "sea" and the "earth" *signifies* that the second beast has no divine legitimacy. As Irenæus also explains (See above, p. 15), the AntiChrist is not like other earthly rulers. He is an outlaw, a renegade, with no respect for the laws of God or man.

[101]His understanding that the "horns" on the beast are individual rulers also corresponds to the interpretation he has given concerning Daniel's visions. The AntiChrist is one horn; his false prophet (who probably will claim to be Elijah) is the other.

and set himself forward as king.[102] And the terms, "he spake like a dragon," mean. that he is a deceiver, and not truthful. And the words, "he exercised all the power of the first beast before him, and caused the earth and them which dwell therein to worship the first beast, whose deadly wound was healed," signify that, after the manner of the law of Augustus, by whom the empire of Rome was established, he too will rule and govern, sanctioning everything by it, and taking greater glory to himself.[103]

For this is the fourth beast,[104] whose head was wounded and healed again, in its being broken up or even dishonoured, and partitioned into four crowns; and he then (Antichrist) shall with knavish skill heal it, as it were, and restore it. For this is what is meant by the prophet when he says,

> "He will give life unto the image, and the image of the beast will speak."
> (Revelation 13:15)

For he will act with vigour again, and prove strong by reason of the laws established by him; and he will cause all those who will not worship the image of the beast to be put to death. Here the faith and the patience of the saints will appear, for he says:

> "And he will cause all, both small and great, rich and poor, free and bond, to receive a mark in their right hand or in their forehead; that no man might buy or sell, save he that had the mark, the name of the beast, or the number of his name."
> (Revelation 13:16–17)

For, being full of guile, and exalting himself against the servants of God, with the wish to afflict them and persecute them out of the world, because they give not glory to him, he will order incense-pans to be set up by all everywhere, that no man among the saints

---

[102]Here Hippolytus clearly indicates the AntiChrist will represent himself to be the legitimate messianic king of Israel, Jesus Christ.

[103]Hippolytus is not saying the AntiChrist will revive the laws of the Roman Empire instituted by Augustus, but that, like Augustus, he will institute laws designed to consolidate his power.

[104]Notice Hippolytus understands the "fourth beast" of Daniel 7:7 ff. to be the first beast mentioned in Revelation 13. The vision recorded in Revelation 13, therefore, describes the actions taken by the AntiChrist in establishing his "kingdom."

THE VOICE of ELIJAH

Restoring the hearts of the fathers to the children

Enclosed is the **free offer booklet** that you—or a friend of yours—requested via our website: ***www.voiceofelijah.org***.

If the subject matter interests you, we invite you to read articles posted on our website Library's Reading Room (at ***www.voiceofelijah.org***). We have much more to offer you. If not, please feel free to pass this booklet on to someone who may be interested in Early Church teaching.

The names and addresses input on our website are only used for mailing the requested free offer booklets. If you (or a friend) requested any of our other five free offer booklets, those were more than likely mailed a few weeks ago, around the time this booklet was mailed. We use U.S. Postal Service Bulk Rate mail, which can take up to 4 weeks to deliver.

We only use the addresses provided on our website for the mailing of requested booklets. Once the booklets have been mailed, we do not use the addresses for any other purpose. We do not maintain addresses in a mailing list for future contact nor do we sell contact information to any other organization.

You have received this free booklet because of the tax-deductible contributions of others on your behalf. There is no charge to you for this booklet, but if you would like to contribute to Voice of Elijah, your contributions are welcome and appreciated.

If you are interested in ordering any of our materials, visit our online store at ***www.voiceofelijah.org***. If you would like to obtain copies of our free offer materials for distribution, call our office at 972-635-2021. Our mailing address is:

Voice of Elijah, Inc., P.O. Box 2257, Rockwall, TX 75087-2257.

Thank you for your interest in *The Voice of Elijah*.

may be able to buy or sell without first sacrificing; for this is what is meant by the mark received upon the right hand. And the word—"in their forehead"—indicates that all are crowned, and put on a crown of fire, and not of life, but of death.

For in this wise, too, did Antiochus Epiphanes the king of Syria, the descendant of Alexander of Macedon, devise measures against the Jews. He, too, in the exaltation of his heart, issued a decree in those times, that

> "all should set up shrines before their doors, and sacrifice, and that they should march in procession to the honour of Dionysus, waving chaplets of ivy;"
> (2 Maccabees 6:7b)

and that those who refused obedience should be put to death by strangulation and torture. But he also met his due recompense at the hand of the Lord, the righteous Judge and all-searching God; for he died eaten up of worms. And if one desires to inquire into that more accurately, he will find it recorded in the books of the Maccabees.[105]

50. But now we shall speak of what is before us. For such measures will he, too, devise, seeking to afflict the saints in every way. For the prophet and apostle says:

> "Here is wisdom, Let him that hath understanding count the number of the beast; for it is the number of a man, and his number is six hundred threescore and six."
> (Revelation 13:18)

With respect to his name, it is not in our power to explain it exactly, as the blessed John understood it and was instructed about it, but only to give a conjectural account of it; for when he appears, the blessed one will show us what we seek to know. Yet as far as our doubtful apprehension of the matter goes, we may speak. Many names indeed we find, the letters of which are the equivalent of this number: such as, for instance, the word Titan, an ancient and notable name; or Evanthas, for it too makes up the same number; and many others which might be found.

But, as we have already said, the wound of the first beast was healed, and he (the second beast) was to make the image speak, that is to say, he should be powerful; and it is manifest to all that those who at present still hold the power are Latins. If, then, we take the

---

[105]See 1 Maccabees 1:1–62; 2 Maccabees 5:1–6:42.

name as the name of a single man, it becomes Latinus. Wherefore we ought neither to give it out as if this were certainly his name, nor again ignore the fact that he may not be otherwise designated. *But having the mystery of God in our heart, we ought in fear to keep faithfully what has been told us by the blessed prophets, in order that when those things come to pass, we may be prepared for them, and not deceived.*[106] For when the times advance, he too, of whom these thing are said, will be manifested.

51. But not to confine ourselves to these words and arguments alone, for the purpose of convincing those who love to study the oracles of God, we shall demonstrate the matter by many other proofs. For Daniel says,

> "And these shall escape out of his hand, even Edom, and Moab, and the chief of the children of Ammon."
> (Daniel 11:41)

Ammon and Moab are the children born to Lot by his daughters,[107] and their race survives even now. And Isaiah says:

> "And they shall fly in the boats of strangers, plundering the sea together, and (they shall spoil) them of the east: and they shall lay hands upon Moab first; and the children of Ammon shall first obey them."
> (Isaiah 11:14)

52. In those times, then, he shall arise and meet them. And *when he has overmastered three horns out of the ten in the array of war, and has rooted these out, viz., Egypt, and Libya, and Ethiopia,*[108] *and has got their spoils and trappings, and has brought the remaining horns which suffer into subjection,*[109] *he will begin to be lifted up in heart, and to exalt himself against God as master of the whole world.* And his first expedition will be against Tyre and Berytus,[110] and the circumjacent territory. For by storming these cities first he will strike

---

[106]No more succinct warning could be issued to True Believers.

[107]Genesis 19:37–38.

[108]He gains this information from Daniel 11:43.

[109]This seems to indicate that, by subjugating the other seven horns of the fourth beast of Daniel 7, the AntiChrist will thereby bring into being the second beast of Revelation 13. (See above, p. 20 ff.)

[110]For "Berytus" read "Beirut." Current circumstances in Lebanon could easily contribute to this as a logical first strike.

terror into the others, as Isaiah says,

> "Be thou ashamed, O Sidon; the sea hath spoken, even the strength
> of the sea hath spoken, saying, I travailed not, nor brought forth
> children; neither did I nurse up young men, nor bring up virgins.
> But when the report comes to Egypt, pain shall seize them for
> Tyre."
> (Isaiah 23:4–5)

*53. These things, then, shall be in the future, beloved; and when
the three horns are cut off, he will begin to show himself as God,*[111] as
Ezekiel has said aforetime:

> "Because thy heart has been lifted up, and thou hast said, I am
> God."
> (Ezekiel 28:2)

And to the like effect Isaiah says:

> "For thou hast said in thine heart, I will ascend into heaven, I will
> exalt my throne above the stars of heaven: I will be like the Most
> High. Yet now thou shall be brought down to hell (Hades), to the
> foundations of the earth."
> (Isaiah 14:13–15)

In like manner also Ezekiel:

> "Wilt thou yet say to those who slay thee, I am God? But thou (shalt
> be) a man, and no God."
> (Ezekiel 28:9)

* * * * * *[112]

60. Now, concerning the tribulation of the persecution which is
to fall upon the Church from the adversary, John also speaks thus:

---

[111]Hippolytus has here extracted those passages the Church has tradi-
tionally applied to Satan. Now you can see how they apply. But notice
also that the AntiChrist cannot become the "abomination of desolation"
until after his campaign against the rulers of Egypt, Libya, and Ethiopia
(the Sudan) has paved the way for his rebuilding of the temple in Jerusalem. Only then will he "begin to show himself as God."
[112]In the section omitted here, Hippolytus explains a bit more about how
the AntiChrist will exalt himself as God.

"And I saw a great and wondrous sign in heaven; a woman clothed with the sun, and the moon under her feet, and upon her head a crown of twelve stars. And she, being with child, cries, travailing in birth, and pained to be delivered. And the dragon stood before the woman which was ready to be delivered, for to devour her child as soon as it was born. And she brought forth a man-child, who is to rule all the nations: and the child was caught up unto God and to His throne. And the woman fled into the wilderness, where she hath the place prepared of God, that they should feed her there a thousand two hundred and threescore days.... And then when the dragon saw it, he persecuted the woman which brought forth the man-*child*. And to the woman were given two wings of the great eagle, that she might fly into the wilderness, where she is nourished for a time, and times, and half a time, from the face of the serpent. And the serpent cast (out of his mouth water as a flood after the woman, that he might cause her to be carried away of the flood. And the earth helped the woman, and opened her mouth, and swallowed up the flood which the dragon cast) out of his mouth. And the dragon was wroth with the woman, and went to make war with the saints of her seed, which keep the commandments of God, and have the testimony of Jesus."
(Revelation 12:1–6, 13–17)[113]

61. By the "woman then clothed with the sun," he meant most manifestly the Church, endued with the Father's word, whose brightness is above the sun. And by "the moon under her feet" he referred to her being adorned, like the moon, with heavenly glory. And the words, "upon her head a crown of twelve stars," refer to the twelve apostles by whom the Church was founded. And those, "she, being with child, cries, travailing in birth, and pained to be delivered," mean that the Church will not cease to bear from her heart the Word that is persecuted by the unbelieving in the world. "And she brought forth," he says, "a man-child, who is to rule all the nations;" by which is meant that the Church, always bringing forth Christ, the perfect man-child of God, who is declared to be God and man, becomes the instructor of all the nations.

[113]Notice that the events described in Revelation 12 occur after the death of the two witnesses in Revelation 11 and after the restoration of the beast as described in Revelation 13. Therefore, there is, in these chapters, an overlapping of details.

And the words, "her child was caught up unto God and to His throne," signify that he who is always born of her is a heavenly king, and not an earthly; even as David also declared of old when he said,

> "The Lord said unto my Lord, Sit Thou at my right hand, until I make Thine enemies Thy footstool."
> (Psalms 110:1)

> "And the dragon,"

he says,

> "saw and persecuted the woman which brought forth the man-child. And to the woman were given two wings of the great eagle, that she might fly into the wilderness, where she is nourished for a time, and times, and half a time, from the face of the serpent."
> (Revelation 12:13–14)

That refers to the one thousand two hundred and threescore days (the half of the week) during which the tyrant is to reign and persecute the Church,[114] *which flees from city to city, and seeks concealment in the wilderness among the mountains, possessed of no other defence than the two wings of the great eagle, that is to say, the faith of Jesus Christ*, who, in stretching forth His holy hands on the holy tree, unfolded two wings, the right and the left, and called to Him all who believed upon Him, and covered them as a hen her chickens. For by the mouth of Malachi also He speaks thus:

> "And unto you that fear my name shall the Sun of righteousness arise with healing in His wings."
> (Malachi 4:2)

62. The Lord also says,

> "when ye shall see *the abomination of desolation* stand in the holy place (whoso readeth, let him understand), then let them which be in Judea flee into the mountains, and let him which is on the house-top not come down to take his clothes; neither let him which is in the field return back to take anything, out of his house. And woe unto them that art with child, and to them that give suck, in those days for then shall be great tribulation, such as was not since the

---

[114]From what has been stated previously, we know this describes the last half of the week, after the death of the two witnesses, those he calls Enoch and Elijah.

beginning of the world. And except those days should be short-
ened, there should no flesh be saved."[115]
(Matthew 24:15–22)

And Daniel says,

"And they shall place the abomination of desolation a thousand two
hundred and ninety days. Blessed is he that waiteth, and cometh to
the thousand two hundred and ninety-five days."
(Daniel 12:11–12)[116]

63. And the blessed Apostle Paul, writing to the Thessalonians,
says:

"Now we beseech you, brethren, concerning the coming of our
Lord Jesus Christ, and our gathering together at it, that ye be not
soon shaken in mind, or be troubled, neither by spirit, nor by word,
nor by letters as from us, as that the day of the Lord is at hand. Let
no man deceive you by any means; for (that day shall not come)
except there come the falling away first, and that man of sin be
revealed, the son of perdition, who opposeth and exalteth himself
above all that is called God, or that is worshipped: so that he sitteth
in the temple of God, showing himself that he is God. Remember
ye not, that when I was yet with you, I told you these things? And
now ye know what withholdeth, that he might be revealed in his
time. For the mystery of iniquity doth already work; only he who
now letteth (will let), until he be taken out of the way. And then
shall that wicked be revealed, whom the Lord Jesus shall consume
with the Spirit of His mouth, and shall destroy with the brightness
of His coming: (even him) whose coming is after the working of
Satan, with all power, and signs, and lying wonders, and with all
deceivableness of unrighteousness in them that perish; because
they received not the love of the truth. And for this cause God shall
send them strong delusion, that they should believe a lie: that they

---

[115]He has connected the events Jesus describes in Matthew 24 with the
ministry of Elijah described in Malachi 3 and 4.

[116]Now he has linked the "insight" granted to "the many" of Daniel 12
together with Elijah, the second forerunner of Jesus Christ, and the
events described in Matthew 24. Notice also, however, that he has either
misquoted Daniel 12:12, or an unknown copyist has copied the number
in error. Hippolytus had access to the true number (1,335). He quotes it
correctly in his *Commentary on the Book of Daniel* which is included in *The
Advent of Christ and AntiChrist*.

all might be damned who believed not the truth, but had pleasure in unrighteousness."[117]
(2 Thessalonians 2:1–12)

And Isaiah says,

"Let the wicked be cut off, that he behold not the glory of the Lord."
(Isaiah 26:10)

64. *These things, then, being to come to pass, beloved, and the one week being divided into two parts, and the abomination of desolation being manifested then, and the two prophets and forerunners of the Lord having finished their course, and the whole world finally approaching the consummation, what remains but the coming of our Lord and Saviour Jesus Christ from heaven, for whom we have looked in hope?* who shall bring the conflagration and just judgment upon all who have refused to believe on Him. For the Lord says,

"And when these things begin to come to pass, then look up, and lift up your heads; for your redemption draweth nigh."
(Luke 21:28)

"And there shall not a hair of your head perish."
(Luke 21:18)

"For as the lightning cometh out of the east, and shineth even unto the west, so shall also the coming of the Son of man be. For wheresoever the carcase is, there will the eagles be gathered together."
(Matthew 24:27–28)

* * * * * *

67. These things, then, I have set shortly before thee, O Theophilus, *drawing them from Scripture itself,* in order that, maintaining in

---

[117]Finally, Hippolytus has linked the following things for us,
1) Paul's description of the AntiChrist in 2 Thessalonians; with
2) Malachi's description of the coming of Elijah in Malachi 3–4;
3) the statements Jesus makes concerning the "abomination of desolation" in Matthew 24;
4) the "insight" granted to "the many" in Daniel 12; and
5) the ministry of the two witnesses, one of whom is *parabolically* called Elijah, in Revelation 11.

Taken all together, these Scriptures provide the basis for his knowledge concerning the advent of the AntiChrist.

faith what is written, and anticipating the things that are to be, thou mayest keep thyself void of offence both toward God and toward men, "looking for that blessed hope and appearing of our God and Saviour,"[118] when, having raised the saints among us, He will rejoice with them, glorifying the Father. To Him be the glory unto the endless ages of the ages.

Amen.

---

[118]Titus 2:13.

Summary and Conclusion

In presenting the foregoing information, I have attempted to acquaint you with just a small part of the rich heritage of the Church that Christians have ignored for centuries simply because they have considered it too "primitive" or "unsophisticated" for "modern" categories of thought. However, of all the documents of the Early Church, these works contain some of the most relevant information for our own time. Furthermore, there is much more information we can, and will, cull from the writings of the Early Church Fathers in days and years to come.

First, I introduced you to Irenæus, a disciple of Polycarp who is best known for his monumental second-century work *Against Heresies*, in which he based his refutation of Christian heretics on one simple premise: The Church received its understanding of the Scriptures from the Apostles as a tradition that had been *handed down* from one generation of Church leaders to the next. He forcefully argued the leaders of the Church in his time agreed there was only one *Teaching*. The heretics, on the other hand, agreed on little. They disclosed themselves to be heretics by the fact that they held no common teaching. In Irenæus we found an individual who was highly unlikely to have intentionally modified *The Teaching* in any way.

Then, I introduced you to Hippolytus, a disciple of Irenæus. In his *Treatise on Christ and AntiChrist*, which he wrote for the benefit of his disciple Theophilus, he expressed the same view of the ministry as his Teacher, Irenæus. In this letter, he admonished Theophilus to find other godly Believers to whom he could teach the things he had been taught. In so doing, he quoted the admonishment of Paul to his disciple Timothy:

You therefore, my son, be strong in the grace that is in Christ Jesus. And *the things which you have heard from me in the presence of many witnesses, these entrust to faithful men, who will be able to teach others also.*
(2 Timothy 2:1–2)

So it was obvious Hippolytus was likewise not an individual who would have been likely to distort the *apostolic tradition* he had *received* from his Teacher Irenæus. Therefore, we logically inferred that the things Irenæus and Hippolytus have to say concerning the AntiChrist must reflect those things the Apostle John taught Polycarp. If that be so—and its accuracy can hardly be denied without denying the very foundations of Christianity—then we should treat what they have to say with the utmost respect. That is all the more imperative because, in the Book of Revelation, their spiritual father the Apostle John describes a series of visions he saw in which the final events of history are described symbolically. Those visions include a description of the events leading up to and including the reign of the AntiChrist.

Here is a summary of the pertinent things these two men— Irenæus and Hippolytus—have said about the AntiChrist who will reign on the Earth before the Return of Jesus Christ.

IRENÆUS:
AGAINST HERESIES (V, 19–36)

Irenæus argued that the multiplicity of "Christian" doctrine has its source in Satan, the Liar. Satan has promoted false teaching in the Church because he seeks to be worshiped as God. Through false doctrine he has managed to divert the worship of men from the God Who is and focus it on a god who exists only in the minds of the heretics. By distorting the ideas men have about God, Satan is able to channel the worship of God to himself. He can claim that worship as his own because such people are not actually worshiping God; they are worshiping a figment of their imagination. Therefore, as far as Irenæus is concerned, the heretics, although they claim to worship God, actually worship Satan.

Irenæus goes on to say that the events of the final days will demonstrate the great lengths to which Satan will go in his attempt to be worshiped as God. He will come as a man—the AntiChrist—

for the specific purpose of being proclaimed the messianic king of the Jews. He will then "set himself forth as God" and take his seat in the rebuilt temple in Jerusalem "leading astray those who worship him, as if he were Christ." Irenæus clearly states the "abomination of desolation" spoken of by Daniel and mentioned by Jesus in Matthew 24:15 is Satan sitting in the rebuilt temple of God in Jerusalem, pretending to be God. He indicates that event will take place in the middle of the final seven-year period ("week") before the Return of Jesus Christ.

Irenæus understands the AntiChrist will rise up as a "little horn" among ten kings that rule over ten nations that issue forth from the ancient Roman Empire. The AntiChrist will slay three rulers of those ten (Irenæus doesn't say which three) and be an eighth among the remaining seven. Although these seven rulers "give their power to the beast" (which is the revived Roman Empire), they will not be completely united and therefore, will ultimately come to ruin. Their complete destruction will occur at the time of the Return of Jesus Christ.

One significant thing to note about Irenæus' discussion of the AntiChrist is the fact that it is a part of a much larger discussion in which he explains how and why Satan deceives mankind. He states that Satan "is anxious to be adored as God" and "wishes himself to be proclaimed as king." His point is that Satan will achieve these goals during his reign as the AntiChrist. He specifically says that, in passing off his ultimate deception on the world in the person of the AntiChrist, Satan will pretend to be "the Christ" and "set himself forth as God."

A second significant element in Irenæus' discussion is the fact that he understands the AntiChrist will appear in the middle of the final week and will reign for just three and one-half years. He will suddenly manifest himself while many (in the Church?) are proclaiming "peace and safety," and he will, during his reign, bring about a total destruction of the Earth. He and the other seven rulers with him will "lay Babylon[119] waste, and burn her with fire, and . . . put the Church to flight." By this last statement, Irenæus indicates he

---

[119]As I have stated previously, the *Mystery Babylon* of Revelation 17–18 is this present civilization. (See "Is Iraq Mystery Babylon?" in *The Voice of Elijah*, January 1991.)

understands the Body of Christ—True Believers—will be made to endure the AntiChrist's persecution.

HIPPOLYTUS:
TREATISE ON CHRIST AND ANTICHRIST

In his *Treatise on Christ and AntiChrist*, Hippolytus put together an explanation of the topic for the benefit of his disciple Theophilus. His Teacher Irenæus had explained the manifestation of the Anti-Christ from the perspective of Satan's desire to be worshiped as God, and rule as king (first over the Jews, but ultimately over the entire world). Hippolytus, however, explained it as Satan's desire to *make himself like* Jesus Christ, the Son of God. There is not necessarily any contradiction between their two viewpoints. Christians have always understood that Jesus Christ is God. Furthermore, both men understand Satan will take his seat as a man in the rebuilt temple in Jerusalem, seeking to be worshiped as God, and pretending to be the legitimate messianic king of the Jews, that is, Jesus Christ.

Hippolytus gives a list of those ways in which Satan will, as the AntiChrist, *make himself like* Jesus Christ. In *parabolic* terminology, he says the AntiChrist will rebuild the temple in Jerusalem to emulate the fact that Jesus Christ "built the house"[120] of God through His resurrection. The AntiChrist will also become a king, the king of the Jews, patterning himself after Jesus Christ, the legitimate messianic king of Israel.

When the AntiChrist appears, "he will make himself like the Son of God, and set himself forward as king." After defeating the "three horns out of the ten" (which Hippolytus again identifies as Egypt, Libya, and Ethiopia) and subjugating the remaining seven, the AntiChrist "will begin to be lifted up in heart, and to exalt himself against God as the master of the whole world. And his first expedition will be against Tyre and Beirut." After that, "when the three horns are cut off, he will begin to show himself as God." At that time, he "will begin to despatch missives against the saints, commanding to cut them all off everywhere, on the ground of their refusal to rev-

---

[120]See the explanation of this idiom in the third volume of the Resurrection Theology Series, *House of Israel, Temple of God*.